The Social Media Diet

The Social Media Diet

Helping Young People to Be Smart Consumers Online

Jim Wasserman and Jiab Wasserman

ROWMAN & LITTLEFIELD
Lanham • Boulder • New York • London

Published by Rowman & Littlefield
An imprint of The Rowman & Littlefield Publishing Group, Inc.
4501 Forbes Boulevard, Suite 200, Lanham, Maryland 20706
www.rowman.com

86-90 Paul Street, London EC2A 4NE

Copyright © 2024 by Jim Wasserman and Jiab Wasserman

All rights reserved. No part of this book may be reproduced in any form or by any electronic or mechanical means, including information storage and retrieval systems, without written permission from the publisher, except by a reviewer who may quote passages in a review.

British Library Cataloguing in Publication Information available

Library of Congress Cataloging-in-Publication Data

Names: Wasserman, Jim, 1961- author. | Wasserman, Jiab, author.
Title: The social media diet : helping young people to be smart consumers online / Jim Wasserman and Jiab Wasserman.
Description: Lanham, Maryland : Rowman & Littlefield, [2023] | Includes bibliographical references. | Summary: "As youth are first learning about both the outside world and form identities, the online world suggests answers that may or may not be right for them. Teachers and parents can help kids become aware of these forces that influence kids online, from peers in social apps to influencers in videos. Just as they learn to consider the nutritional value of food choices, The Social Media Diet empowers youth to do the same for online messaging served to their minds" — Provided by publisher.
Identifiers: LCCN 2023035740 (print) | LCCN 2023035741 (ebook) | ISBN 9781475869576 (cloth) | ISBN 9781475869583 (paperback) | ISBN 9781475869590 (epub)
Subjects: LCSH: Education--Computer network resources. | Internet and children. | Internet and teenagers. | Mass media and youth. | Internet—Safety measures. | Computer crimes—Prevention. | Cyberspace—Social aspects.
Classification: LCC LB1044.87 .W377 2023 (print) | LCC LB1044.87 (ebook) | DDC 371.33/4—dc23/eng/20230831
LC record available at https://lccn.loc.gov/2023035740
LC ebook record available at https://lccn.loc.gov/2023035741

Contents

Preface		vii
Introduction		xi
1	New World, Old Problem	1
2	Getting the Lay of the Virtual Land	11
3	Nudges and Sways in the Online World	31
4	Stubborn Things (Fact-Checking Online)	65
5	Chat Talk	97
6	How Influencers Hold Sway	127
7	The Parasocial Relationship	159
Afterword		177
Glossary		179
Bibliography		187
About the Authors		191

Preface

During my thirty-year teaching career, one yearly lesson stood out, the Junior Research Paper, or JURP. For two to three months, high schoolers were asked to go through each stage of formulating a thesis, researching, writing, and editing a college-like seven-to-ten-page paper. It became a rite of passage. When I started in the 1990s, I had to require students to find two "electronic sources," much to their complaining that hard copies were easier. By the time I retired, it was the reverse.

The online world came into its own during that time. Communication and connection changed in form and scope. Kids stopped passing notes—they texted. Students didn't talk about their best friend at camp but how many *friends* and *followers* they had online.[1] Life for them became worldwide. Kids got older, younger.

The advantages of online access have always outweighed the negatives. Students can find news from many perspectives. They can connect with others to learn about and advocate for change. Kids make connections across the globe with people like them, reinforcing their developing self-identity.

Unfortunately, a digital divide also arose. That phrase was mostly and rightly used to distinguish people who had access to the internet from those who didn't. Within the access community, however, another divide occurred: those who felt immediately comfortable with the internet and those who were hesitant to merge the worlds so quickly. The former included many students, the latter many teachers.

To my mind, both sides need each other. Students might be familiar with the internet, but their inexperience with human nature causes them to make many of the same mistakes online as in real life, or IRL as it came to be known.[2] Teachers who summarily dismiss online activity do so mostly out of ignorant fear of the new and unknown. They fail to see how the very same tides of history or human condition found in the literature they teach also plays out in cyberspace. Social media is just the newest forum for human interaction and drama, including people seeking to make connections, seeking companionship, sharing gossip, sharing accurate and inaccurate information, and otherwise trying to have their existence, perspectives, and worth validated.

While I was teaching, my wife and partner, Jiab, was working in the banking and financial world. Over that same time, she saw how those who had learned the skills to understand and adapt to evolving tech thrived. On the other hand, those who were ill-prepared fell behind the march of progress. They even became financially susceptible to predatory scams.

Together, Jiab and I see the internet as a wonderful tool that enhances lives. Like any tool, however, it is best wielded by someone trained in its use. For all the times we adults solve a problem with a conscious thought of "Wow, I'm glad I was taught about that," there are a hundred other times we have the same good fortune but don't realize how education prepared us to make the right choice. If we are taught good nutrition, we tend to start having "gut"—pun intended—feelings that some things are better not digested. We also learn to positively consume things that make life longer, richer, and even more fun.

That is our goal with this book. The internet has evolved over the last thirty years from tech novelty to ubiquity. Kids today grow up from birth with the real life and the internet as dual worlds with one foot, eyeball, and texting hand in each, often at the same time. We want to empower youth to become active information nutritionists for their minds. We also want to assist teachers, counselors, and parents to learn about the online world youth grow up in and how they, as experienced adults, can help prepare kids for success in both worlds.

One final note: We started this book centered around teaching kids how to make good choices online. True to our concept of overlapping worlds, we discovered that so much needed to be also said about the general nature of how kids make choices in any case, IRL or online. That compelled us to write a companion book, *Behavioral Economics: A Guide for Youth in Making Choices.* It investigates both the internal motivators and external nudges and sways on youth decision-making.[3] We invite you to read it.

Jim Wasserman

NOTES

1. In a wonderful display of typical teen spirit, Facebook was so distracting initially that my school blocked it. The students, before smartphones, used their computers to go to FB England. The school then blocked all FB sites in English. The kids then went to FB portals in other languages because the page layout and buttons were the same. Kids will be kids.

2. Early on, experts talked of "digital natives" and "digital immigrants." It was a ham-fisted overgeneralization. Born in the 1960s, I was a "TV native," yet in my youth I could neither explain how a TV worked internally nor distinguish which ads on TV were trustworthy.

3. When we refer in this book to a concept explored in the first book, we provide a short summary.

Introduction

This book at first glance seems just for teachers. It is primarily written for classroom use. In a broader sense, however, it is also designed for anyone who wants to help youth develop skills to successfully navigate the cyberspace that coexists in their lives with the real world, including social media. To that end, we have included a lot of vocabulary and explanations of cyberspace so that anyone, including educators, parents, and counselors, can understand the lay of the cyber landscape that new app and internet explorers face.

We focus on where kids hang out the most, but one must keep in mind that there are really no gatekeepers to ensure that young users interact with social peers. One theme running through this book is that the online space is pretty much one big sandbox where anyone can play. There isn't a restricted area online for kids that keeps adult predators out, or a trustful bouncer at the door that ensures that kids behave cordially or only have access to age appropriate material.

Before we tell you more about what we are doing in this book, let us say two things we do *not* do here.

We do not present kids' online life in purely theoretical or formal pedological terms.

Teachers, of course, know their stuff. That doesn't mean, however, they want their resource material presented to them in overly esoteric, academic terms.

Teachers are multitasking with many students from the moment class starts. For a complicated topic like kids being online, they need the equivalent of a plug-and-play accessory rather than the intricate components of raw theory that they are then expected to assemble into working devices in their "spare time." For every concept we present here, we strive to put it in easy-to-communicate terms so teachers—and parents, counselors, and even kids themselves—can quickly grasp the concept and then dive deeper into it.

We do not lay out an entire new course of study, but rather a supplement to existing subject matter.

Every teacher has been asked why they do not include something extra in their curriculum, such as other novels, another part of history or geography, personal finance, or a litany of practical life skills. They are all good ideas, but they ignore that the curriculum space is already filled up.

Every teacher is an economist. They are experts at efficient use of the scarcest resource, time. Any suggestion to include more topics or material, including media literacy, induces consternation. So, we have designed lessons in this book that cover media literacy while also overlapping as much as possible with already-established subjects, such as writing or math. The lessons can thus serve a dual purpose rather than being a diversion from what often is required by state mandates. We focus on something universal to all aspects of being online and in the real world: the skills of choice-making.[1]

We also have tried not to make this book a list of "Thou shalt / shalt not . . ." for adults to pass on to youth. That is an ineffective way to instruct. Rather, our approach is to outline principles and concepts that young people can then apply in their daily lives. As we will repeatedly say, in many ways it is like teaching about good nutrition. It's impossible to designate all foods as "consume" or "don't consume." It's better to teach principles of healthy consumption and leave it to young people to apply those principles in their choices of food and ingredients. We believe the same approach works for healthy consumption of messaging and social media.

Along those same lines, allow us to share a situation that arose as we wrote this book in mid-2023. Just as we were finishing, there seemed to be an awakening within government as to the potential harm of allowing people unfettered access to social apps. The focus was particularly keen on TikTok for its privacy and data extraction dangers. Several states banned employees from having the app on government-issued devices. One state banned new downloads of TikTok within its borders. The US Congress had hearings with app leaders and industry experts while mulling over new regulation.

While we applauded the government's awakening to the topic of apps and online danger, we were panicked by the thought of having to rewrite whole sections of this book in light of new regulations and possible banning. Meanwhile, ByteDance, the parent company of TikTok, was preparing to roll out a new app, Lemon8, in case legislators made good on their threats.

It was that preparation that gave us clarity. For us to reedit every time the app and online players changed would be playing whack-a-mole. History further shows that government prohibitions on societal corruption are at best a Band-Aid on the problem, whether the war on drugs in the late twentieth century, Prohibition in the early twentieth century, or even the Puritan war on sports and gaming in the seventeenth century.

We support government action to protect online users, especially youth. Our focus for a better cyber world, however, is on educating and empowering users themselves. We don't mean a simplified "Just say no" campaign. We believe that apps and online sites, which can be used for good or bad, will be around for a long time. Therefore, what we advocate is educating youth to be smart consumers of such experiences and to develop skills that help them to make good choices. We also want to encourage people to reflect on why they are drawn to such diversions from real life. By understanding the root causes of their desire to engage online, they will make better, healthier choices.

In the end, it is less important if the latest cyber quicksand is TikTok, Lemon8, or another site or platform that comes out between the time we write this and when you read it. The fundamental skills needed by users are the same, even if the names change.

You will find that each chapter, as it examines a topic, provides *exploratories* for youth to see how the concepts we cover play out in the real world. We don't want students to just think about what we tell them about being online and in apps, but to think about what *they* see. Is it the same or different from the way we describe it or the way others experience it? If so, how and, most importantly, *why*?

The exploratories in this book are not designed to be airtight clinical investigations free of confounding variables. Our goal is to give students who are first learning about being online a simple, visceral experience. We want them to have fun, to have a freedom to wander and wonder that will carry the learning forward.

Feel free to modify the exploratories as best fits your young explorers. We provide several follow-up questions covering what we hope is a wide variety of topics and ideas for a spectrum of ages. For advanced students, feel free to encourage some extra thoughtful thinking afterward, such as "What could be changed in the exploratory that might yield a different result?" If an exploratory goes wrong, ask why it did so and what could be done next time.

Counselors, parents, and anyone else who wants to promote online skills will find the topics and lessons in the book accessible and fun to do with youth. We need to better prepare the next generation for online choice-making that we can't even imagine today. Because it's not about what the messengers say or the sways that push a child's identity and development in a given direction; it's about empowering kids so that they are prepared to think critically. Then, they can choose for themselves who they want to be and, to borrow from Dr. Seuss, the places they'll go.

NOTE

1. Like teachers confined by time, we also have limited space to cover all skills youth need to be successful online. We have had to choose some areas of media and online literacy to omit. Some want students to have more technical training, such as how to make a podcast; others want a study of communication. Would that it all could be included in this book, but it can't.

Chapter One

New World, Old Problem

About twenty years into the turn of the century, there occurred a society-wide disruption. New technology was changing how people communicated, got information, and even lived. New social networks were replacing old ones; homes were being redesigned and rewired to accommodate the change.

Young people were especially embracing and mastering the new electronics, connecting in new ways that adults were not even aware of. When parents were aware, they were confused and worried. The new way of socializing took up too much of their children's attention. Oldsters saw distance connection as a poor substitute for the face-to-face socialization they had growing up. It was perhaps even dangerous. Might it harm their children long-term?

Of course, what we are talking about is the turn of the twentieth century. The new, radical technology was . . . the telephone.

Patented by Alexander Graham Bell in 1876, the telephone took off in the early 1900s and, after a pause in growth due to World War I, became a household fixture by the 1920s. Homes were designed to include a phone nook. Formerly face-to-face chats were now done by way of the "blower." Teens, who before conducted their socializing, or "courting," under watchful parental eyes, could now talk over distance and even in secret.[1]

As teen subculture began to form, so did teen slang. A young man could try to *pitch woo* about *making whoopee* to a *flapper* he thought was the *bee's knees* on the *horn*, at least until she told him to *dust out* and *breeze off* because he gave her the *heebie-jeebies*. Best he *23 skidoo*.[2]

Society had to adapt to accept that the telephone and distant socialization was something that was not going away.[3] Somehow, the in-person world and the phone world would have to coexist. Even the initial greeting had to be worked out. Alexander Graham Bell wanted people to say "Ahoy!" like on a ship. Most people settled for "Hello," but some felt it wasted time. Rather, it became polite to answer by saying one's telephone number, so that the caller would know they got the right number.[4] Of course, the caller should then immediately identify themself.[5] And all this was before the conversation really started!

There were also unforeseen problems, even traps, that arose as the telephone became ubiquitous. How early or late was it polite to call someone? (The informal rule came to be between 9:00 a.m. and 9:00 p.m.) Without seeing someone's face when talking, how could we know when the speaker was joking or that we might have misheard them? Worst of all, scammers and other people with ill intent were finding ways to use the new device to trick people out of money or to come to dangerous rendezvous by pretending to be someone they were not.

One hundred years later, many more technologies and innovations have changed society or required new rules. Some people profess confusion and predict societal ruin with each leap forward. Society, including the technological doubters, eventually adapt and continue to move forward.

Still, whenever new technology is first introduced, there are no guidelines, rules, or best practices.[6] What becomes standard practice is often laid down by the government or other supervising authority by way of regulation as issues arise.[7] The other way procedures and customs arise is by **crowdsourcing**. That is when a large number of people all contribute information or opinions, from which a general view, opinion, or practice arises.[8] The custom of saying "hello" when answering the phone arose because of crowdsourcing.

See **Lesson 1A: Check the Tech**.

Authority-devised rules and crowdsourcing can be great ways to create practices and customs together. If the authority uses experts, they can see the big picture to do what's best for the most people or to create a uniform way of doing things. They can also see problems the average person might not be aware of, like scammers using tech to hurt people. On the other hand, crowdsourcing gives the users the control to immediately shape the tech's use in a way that fits their wants or needs.

See **Lesson 1B: Three's a Crowdsource**.

This is not a book about the 1900s and telephones—a bit late for that. It's about the 2000s and the internet. As the saying goes, however, the more things change, the more they stay the same.

The internet and world of social apps may seem old and well established to youth of today.[9] It's still new, however, and still being formed. It will continue to be revised and rebuilt just as with the phone. Government regulators and other overseers are creating rules and regulations.[10] At the same time, users crowdsource to personalize the online world's benefits.[11] Even with both, however, there are many traps and dangers that we cannot see or don't have a good answer for. It's therefore important that users of the internet and apps, whether to visit sites, watch videos, or chat with friends, need to be aware of those traps and dangers.

See **Lesson 1C: 28.3495 Grams of Prevention**.

If the internet is a place to wander, wonder, and yet be wary even for the average adult, imagine how much more so it is for young users venturing into it today. Tweens and early teens are already trying to digest all the messages and possibilities of their small corner of the real world. Imagine the brain overload of the internet bringing the rest of the world to them virtually all at once. Young people go from interacting with a few people, usually people their age, to now interacting with potentially people of all ages, experience, and intent online. It's like kids who have just mastered the rules of the local kiddie pool are suddenly thrown into the ocean.

Some kids already know this experience indirectly by way of gaming, in particular role-playing games (RPGs). When one first starts an RPG, the first task is often to create a version of one's self for the game, called an **avatar**. The gamer can make the avatar look like them, or they can try out a whole new look, body build, gender, or whatever suits their fancy. Once they then enter the game's world, they must figure out the "physics" of that game space. Can they jump or run and, if so, how far? What tools can they use? How can they get hurt? How can they succeed? What is of value or "currency" and how can it be earned or lost? Who are friends and who are foes? Who can be trusted?

With one's avatar, a player can experiment, even try crazy, risky, or outright dangerous things within the game. They can also try out different personalities. The quiet person IRL can try being the loud smasher who will not be ignored in the game world. That's because the danger is only to one's avatar within the game.[12] If things don't go the gamer's way, the gamer can reset and retry.

That risk-taking without permanent loss may not exist outside the game. It certainly is not always the way IRL, and often is not so interacting online. A noob[13] can have their in-game gold stolen or their character wiped out. Online and in social apps, real money, even one's identity, can be stolen. Say the wrong thing to an NPC[14] and they may not cooperate with you or give you the best deal. Say the wrong thing to a real person online and friendships and reputations can be destroyed. What happens online easily flows over into the real, physical world, with real-life, and real harm, consequences.[15]

See **Lesson 1D: Hey Now, You're an Avatar**.

NOTES

1. The simultaneous rise of the automobile's popularity also allowed for teen freedom. Many sociologists consider the Roaring Twenties the beginning of modern teen-dom, along with conventions such as replacing courtship with casual dating.
2. We'll leave you to figure out what all that *jazz* and *jive* slang means.
3. Of course, letter-writing remained, but the phone's ability for instant connection and technological panache made it an entirely new form.
4. In case you have forgotten, old telephones did not display the number the dialer called.
5. Since the introduction of caller ID, only we oldsters still do that.
6. In philosophy, a world that is yet unbuilt or unstructured is called the *state of nature*. Philosophers such as Thomas Hobbes and John Locke debated how people would act in a state of nature. Would we be kind? Would we cooperate? Would we be selfish and only look out for ourselves?
7. In the early days of addressing when multiple cars came to intersections, some states initially passed laws that said a driver must let the other car go first. Right-of-way laws were eventually revised, presumably after long lineups of polite, obedient motorists at intersections.
8. In much the same way, laws in England historically were from two sources. One was statutory law that was created by government bodies like Parliament. The other was after years of custom or court cases that made it a law, such as that your doctor can't tell others what they know about your health. It's called *common law*, but it really is crowdsourcing over generations.
9. If kids today know of ancient cyberspaces such as Myspace, which as of this book's writing is still around, it is probably through parental reminiscing.
10. Today, it's hard to imagine the 1980s, when site creators gave their cyberspaces random domain names, until 1994, when the current URL system of domain name and file path, with separating syntax of /, \, and . was universally initiated.
11. Although based on the concept of a single person, Wikipedia's contents and popularity are attributed to crowdsourcing.
12. The hidden IRL dangers behind gaming, including bullying, identity theft, and money sapping, are not considered for this point but will be addressed later.
13. A gaming term for a new person to a game, often inexperienced with low knowledge within the game. They can sometimes be taken advantage of by more-experienced gamers.
14. Short for a nonplaying character, or a character built into the game that a player interacts with, such as a shop clerk who sells weapons and armor.
15. One distinction between gaming and IRL/online is that in the gaming world, one's level is usually on display. A new entrant (level 1) can avoid a level 10 opponent. IRL, levels are not shown but society tries to keep kids interacting with those similar in experience level to them. Online, it's an open mix and anyone can pretend to be any level, even to their or others' harm.

Chapter 1 Accompanying Lessons

LESSON 1A: CHECK THE TECH

Focus of Exploration

How technology changes lives

Intro Questions/Thoughts for Students

How has tech changed your life? Look around wherever you are as you read this and ask what wasn't around twenty-five years ago? Fifty? A hundred? How might your life be different without it?

Activity

Walk around your home or think of major technological innovations that changed society, such as the telephone, the airplane, television, air-conditioning, the internet, or the smartphone.

Think about how you would have done the same things you do now—schoolwork, make arrangements, or hang out with friends—before that technology came about. Look for photos or descriptions of people doing what you do now but before the technology you use. If you can, interview older people who remember what it was like before the tech. Put it all together in an essay or display.

Follow-Up Questions/Discussions

Would your life have been very different before tech? How? Is it just a matter that things would take more time, or was the quality of life different? How so?

We tend to be thankful for new tech, but can you come up with at least one advantage or way of life that was a bit nicer or easier before the tech came about? Can you re-create that now by choosing some times to go without the tech? Maybe instead of texting, choose to chat in person, or maybe even walk to meet up?

Tech isn't just devices. It can also be new systems. For example, people used to pay in cash, then the credit card system was developed. Now we have online payment apps. What systems do you rely on, and how was life different before they were around?

If you could create the next society-changing tech or system, what would you create? What would be the advantage? What might be lost?

LESSON 1B: THREE'S A CROWDSOURCE

Focus of Exploration

Crowdsourcing

Intro Questions/Thoughts for Students

Do you and your friends have rules or expectations for the people in your group? Are there certain ways you count on people to behave, or things you expect them to do or not do?

How did the expectations or rules come about? Did one person announce them? Did you all discuss it, or did you all just fall into it as an expectation?

Activity

With your friends, list the stated and implied "rules" or expectations of your group. They could be general, like agreeing to listen whenever there is a problem or not publicly embarrassing each other, or specific, such as wearing something or doing a regular activity. For each rule or expectation, try to figure out how you all came to agree by that expectation. Did you discuss it, or did it just arise? Was it in reaction to something specific that came up?

Follow-Up Questions/Discussions

Were most of the rules and expectations that you came up with intentionally created or just came to be? If they just came to be and you all followed them, does that mean you all agree with the rule or expectation?

How would you go about changing a rule or expectation if you wanted to? Would you just stop following it, maybe secretly, or talk it over with some or all of your group? Which is the better method in certain circumstances?

If someone breaks a rule of group expectation, what do you do? Does it matter how serious the rule is? When might you be angry with the other person for breaking the rule, and when might you be concerned that they may need help? What would you do then?

Do you and your friends have different rules or expectations IRL and online? Do your friends or you act differently online, or treat others differently? Do you like that difference? If you don't, what can you do?

Have you ever been part of a crowd that seemed to be deciding things in what you thought was the wrong direction? Maybe they were building up a consensus based on incomplete or bad information, or they were working each other up emotionally. What can you do when that is happening?

LESSON 1C: 28.3495 GRAMS OF PREVENTION

Focus of Exploration

Precautions against traps and dangers IRL and online

Intro Questions/Thoughts for Students

IRL, what are some potential traps and dangers you are aware of that you intentionally avoid? What are your "Wait, be careful!" moments?

Where might there be traps or dangers that you don't know about yet but might exist? What precautions can you take to not fall into traps and dangers you are not aware of?

Activity

For the real world, list the following that help you to avoid falling into traps and dangers:

- Rules that help to keep you out of danger
- Skills you have that help you to avoid or escape traps and danger
- Precautions you take (such as fastening your seat belt) to avoid or minimize future dangers

Now do the same for being online and using social media.

Follow-Up Questions/Discussions

How are the traps and dangers IRL and online similar and how are they different? Are the precautions and skills you use IRL and online the same or different?

We think of dangers as causing immediate harm, but some can be harmful slowly over a long period of time, like a place contaminated with poison. Can you include some places like that both IRL and online? What are the possible long-term dangers? How can you avoid the dangers?

Taking precautions sometimes means giving something up, like not doing a fun activity or going someplace because the risk of harm is too great. How do we balance out the risk of harm versus fun, both IRL and online?

Who are good guides in your life about potential harm, both IRL and online?

LESSON 1D: HEY NOW, YOU'RE AN AVATAR

Focus of Exploration

Designing avatars as a self-reflection

Intro Questions/Thoughts for Students

Do you think your looks reflect who you are on the inside? If you could change your appearance to better reflect how you see yourself, what might you change?

Activity

Gamers often create **avatars** of themselves to operate within the game. Many social apps also allow for creation of an avatar. Using either an animation program, a specific avatar creation site or app, or just drawing, you and your friends and family are to create two avatars each.

For your first avatar, create something that looks how you see your outside self. If you wish, you can place around you objects that might relate to what you do, such as sports equipment, books, or art. Don't put your name on it, but once everyone is done, have people guess who they think each avatar is a depiction of.

For your second avatar, create one that shows your "inner self." It can look the same as your outside, but if you see yourself (or how you envision your future self) differently, depict that. You can also place around you your internal passions. They could be the same as what you already do or they could be different, representing what you would like to try or what you hope your future self will do. Again, don't put names on it and see who can correctly guess who it is.

Follow-Up Questions/Discussions

Were your two avatars very different? Why was there any difference? Was the difference between your present and future, hopeful self, or was it something different?

Was it harder to create one avatar more than the other or the same? Why do you think that is? Was there anything you held back because you did not like it or were embarrassed to depict it? Did you give hints or subtle clues to anything?

In some ways being on social media allows you to create an avatar, or at least a **persona**. Is your social media or other online avatar similar to your personality IRL? How is it different?

On social media, people often choose a picture of themselves or a pet or an animation for their profile picture avatar. What would you choose if you do not have one? If you do, can people see why you chose to use that profile picture? What does it say about you or how you see yourself? Do you make judgments about people based on their profile picture?

If you can, save the avatars you created. Put on a calendar to revisit them in a year. What do you hope will change?

Chapter Two

Getting the Lay of the Virtual Land

There is an informal rule of historical analysis: If you want to understand the impact of an event or innovation, you need to wait about twenty years. That allows the crashing waves of initial impact and then counter-impact to settle some. Most of the people yelling at each other "It changes everything!" and "It changes nothing!" will have settled down. Most of all, it gives analysts time to take a longer view. Time reveals if there will be a permanent, drastic change in society, a slight change in course, or pretty much no change at all.

This is all to say it's way too early to say with any certainty what will be the long-term and permanent impact of COVID-19, the resulting lockdowns, and the societal switch to more online interaction that began in 2020. That won't stop us from trying, however, especially as we need to understand what the online world is today for youth taking their first cyber dives into the mysterious internet waters.

Those primordial waters are churning. Take the word and idea of an **influencer**. You have no doubt heard it more in the last couple of years. Google trends show that interest in the concept, represented by the word's use in Google searches, first began to rise in 2015–2016.[1] Meanwhile, there was an observable increase in overall online activity once the lockdown came. One 2021 study indicated a 17 percent increase in screen use by minors in 2019–2021 compared to the four years before the pandemic.[2]

One would imagine that the idea of an influencer, someone **swaying** people as to cultural tastes and norms—for our purposes mainly through online and social media platforms—would have exploded as people locked down turned to influencers as lifelines to general culture. Sure enough, since March 2020, when the first restrictions began in the United States, there has been a 143 percent increase in use of the word in Google search terms.

See **Lesson 2A: Trend Setting**.

Similarly, the pre-2020 growth of social apps such as Instagram, as well as video platforms like YouTube, saw a continuation of that steady usage at slightly higher rates in 2020 and 2021.[3] TikTok, which launched in 2017, snowballed in popularity by 2020.[4] The actual usage during that time was more even, though it is clear the app came into its own during this time.

One last interesting change in usage concerns Snapchat. People "on the go" use it to record their activities.[5] As might be expected, then, its usage leveled off early in 2020 as people stopped "going" and stayed in. As moving about has reemerged, Snapchat's usage has again taken off.[6]

The online world, especially social apps, remains one dominated by twentysomethings and early thirtysomethings,[7] with teens eagerly getting a running start. Yet, even with all this data and metadata to digest, there is one group largely unaccounted for, and largely unmonitored: youth.[8]

See **Lesson 2B: Staying in Your Age Lane**.

The online world, and how we measure it in the US, was defined by a 1998 law, at least in regard to youth. That was early in the life of the online universe, just after its big bang.[9] Even early on, people saw the potential problem of exploiting naive children online, especially as to secretly watching and recording what they did there. So, the Children's Online Privacy Protection Act (COPPA) was passed that said platforms and websites were not allowed to gather data from users who were under thirteen.[10] Since websites and platforms gather data on all users, it was thought that this would compel them to block children under thirteen from visiting.

If you try to create an account on most social apps today, you can see the resulting "security." The app will extensively grill and examine you with an age-old question, "What year were you born?" If you submit any year older than thirteen years ago, you pass. If you enter any date less than thirteen years ago, you will not be allowed in because, we all know, children would *never* lie. Many websites adopted a similarly non-rigorous test, or even cut out the math by having the user simply click on a box that promises they are of appropriate age for their content.

YouTube reverses the demand for cross-your-heart promises by having the content provider or video uploader identify if the material is geared toward an audience under thirteen. If the content is for kids, YouTube won't collect data without consent from a parent and won't use behavior targeting tactics to show children relevant ads.[11]

So, what does COPPA and the resulting "No Kids Allowed" front-door checks on websites and apps mean, at least as far as knowing what youth are up to online? It means that platforms don't collect data on youth users because, to their stats, there are none. Everyone who visits their site—except

YouTube—has pinky sworn they are of age, even if they have to try a couple of times.[12]

We are getting peeks into under-thirteen-year-old usage and the effects of the lockdown, in-school closings, and switching to online curriculum.[13] Anecdotally, many parents will tell you that the timing for introducing their children to the online world was accelerated. Schools asked many children to access their work online. Parents sought ways to keep their children engaged at home. Children, in their cyber-walking to and back from online school or to parent-authorized sites, inevitably became interested in the general online neighborhood and began to check out other virtual shops and hangout places, some not meant for kids. We won't get a full picture until we can survey today's Gen Aers[14] in a couple of years to ask them when and how they first entered the online world.

See **Lesson 2C: Call Security!**

If the United States is mostly content with knowing that they don't know what youth are up to, the United Kingdom delves more into the situation. Of course, their children's usage may vary from that of American kids, but their numbers are illustrative. Ofcom is the British government's monitoring and regulatory authority for the UK communications industries, including the internet.[15]

In 2021, an Ofcom survey indicated that 25 percent of three-year-olds had a social media profile, according to their parents.[16] That percentage rose to 80 percent for twelve-year olds. Bear in mind that the UK maintains the same thirteen-year-old minimum age for social media apps like Snapchat, Instagram, and Facebook as the US does. Two-thirds of parents surveyed were not aware of the correct minimum age requirements, however, and a large percentage of the parents admitted to setting up accounts for their underage child.

As for the efficacy of the entryway promise that a user is of age, another UK study found that about one-third of social app users between the ages of eight and seventeen claimed they were of adult age, over eighteen, in creating their account.[17] Among the eight-to-twelve age-group, the study estimated that almost two in five (39 percent) had a user age profile of sixteen-plus years old, while just under a quarter (23 percent) claimed a user age of eighteen-plus.

Though not as complete as the British numbers, American usage studies by private groups give us a similar portrait of underage usage.[18] CNN reported in 2021 on a survey that found about half of the parents of children ages ten to twelve said their child used social media apps in the first six months of that year; 32 percent of parents of kids ages seven to nine also reported such usage.[19]

In 2021 Common Sense Media conducted one of the first comprehensive studies to measure online usage by minors after the impact of the lockdown, interviewing the youth themselves.[20] For eight-to-twelve-year-olds, the study found that 38 percent said they had ever used social media, with 18 percent saying they used it every day.[21] Even then, one has to remember that those numbers were only as to social media, not being online as a whole. The survey also found that 64 percent of tweens watch online videos every day and 43 percent play mobile games.

These categories should be taken as fuzzy, however. Gamers can talk and socially interact through many games. Gamers also will play while simultaneously communicating with their fellow gamers on social media such as Discord. Videos have comments sections. Some websites, such as Reddit, can function as both message boards and social media platforms. There are also significant variations by demographics: Boys use more screen media[22] than girls, and children from lower-income households use screen media more than those from higher-income households.[23]

So, what do all these numbers add up to? Basically, the idea that children don't access the internet "that much" is a myth. They are also often unsupervised. As far back as 2013, a Microsoft survey found that parents allowed their children to be online unsupervised beginning, on average, around eight years old.[24] And that's for the parents who know their kids are going online. A now-old term is **finsta**, or fake social media account.[25] Kids with such accounts will probably not reveal having them in surveys or to their parents to then tell.[26] Blogs openly recommend social media accounts underage kids should follow. That many tween-oriented cartoons and programs have social media accounts for their viewers to follow is another indication.[27] It's one big open secret.

See **Lesson 2D: Open Privacy**.

Despite COPPA, the advice of medical experts, and even social media's own studies,[28] youth are actively online, including on social media. They talk to each other about it when not online, and so the entirety of it all amounts to one large societal sway that kids should be online. Thus, the next inquiries are what kids are doing while online and where are they doing it.

The big three consistent activities for tweens are TV/video watching,[29] gaming, and social media.[30] Video and gaming choices vary greatly by personal kid taste. Social media apps, on the other hand, tend to attract large sections of youth in clumps.

Which social media dominates remains a tricky thing to definitively say, however. Facebook remains the largest platform worldwide, but few Gen Aers use it. WhatsApp is one of the most popular apps in the world, but not in the United States. Snapchat seems to be the usage winner among tweens who want to communicate directly with friends, though Instagram also remains popular. TikTok saw perhaps the largest spike of any social media platform during the lockdown. Ofcom's studies seem to confirm TikTok's popularity among underage British users. Again, numbers are hard to gauge with the claimed thirteen-year-old supposed minimum age floor. Other activities, such as content creation and e-reading, ranked in and out of popularity depending on the study.[31]

See **Lesson 2E: Charting a Life of Pie to Raise the Bar**.

Is all of this youth activity online a bad thing? You're probably expecting us to shout out "Yes! Stop it right now!" Like most things, however, a child being online has possible good and bad, like visiting any place does. Being online was an educational lifeline during the lockdown, and there remain many activities that are educational or just fun. Studies show that online social connections, whether casual or over a common hobby or interest, can help social development.[32]

And then there's the downside. As we said before, youth have gone from having their own dedicated swimming pool to being thrown in the general online deep water with the adults. Tweens are exposed to ideas and aspects of the world they are not developmentally ready for.

Aside from potentially bad stuff online, another factor to consider is what economists call the **opportunity cost**. If a person chooses to watch a movie over doing homework, the opportunity cost is perhaps being better prepared for class. The opportunity cost of doing homework is the enjoyment and relaxation missed from watching the movie. During the lockdown, kids had little choice but to be online. Now that the lockdown is lifted, kids need to weigh out what is gained and what is potentially lost from choosing between the online world and activities IRL.

See **Lesson 2F: The Cost of Opportunity**.

We said in the last chapter that when new technology first comes into society, rules and norms are decided by a combination of those with authority and from crowdsourcing. So, where are the authorities to better control, or at least oversee, youth activity on the internet? Leaving it to websites and social apps to self-police, we must remember that it is actually against their own financial interest to block users by strict enforcement. They will usually claim they are trying their best, but that doing so is difficult.[33] Similarly, frustrated parents will tell you they can't monitor their children's activities all the time, and that in any case many children will lie, deceive, and otherwise get around any rules, so what's the point?

That pretty much leaves any tempering of youth wandering a wide-open internet to the kids themselves. There is no single definitive standard that is "best practices" for all youth going online.[34] As a first step, however, parents and children need to have open and honest communication so that they are aware of each other's honest desires, goals, and activities. From there, mutual expectations can be agreed upon as a cooperative adventure. This will also help kids to stand against the many sways and nudges from outside the family, perhaps even sharing with parents and educators the challenges they face to find solutions together in such circumstances.

See **Lesson 2G: Buddy System.**

NOTES

1. Google Trends, "Influencer," n.d., https://trends.google.com/trends/explore?date=all&geo=US&q=influencer.

2. Rafael Maravilla, "Kids as Young as 8 Are Using Social Media More Than Ever, Study Finds," PACEsConnection, March 25, 2022 (originally published in the *New York Times*, March 24, 2022), https://www.pacesconnection.com/blog/kids-as-young-as-8-are-using-social-media-more-than-ever-study-finds-nytimes-com.

3. Mansoor Iqbal, "Instagram Revenue and Usage Statistics (2018)," Business of Apps, March 8, 2021, https://www.businessofapps.com/data/instagram-statistics.

4. Mansoor Iqbal, "TikTok Revenue and Usage Statistics (2021)," Business of Apps, November 11, 2022, https://www.businessofapps.com/data/tik-tok-statistics. TikTok is under review for possibly being heavily regulated, restricted, or even banned by the US government as a security risk. No regulations have been passed as of this writing.

5. Jack Shepherd, "21 Essential Snapchat Statistics You Need to Know in 2022," *The Social Shepherd*, January 3, 2023, https://thesocialshepherd.com/blog/snapchat-statistics.

6. Mansoor Iqbal, "Snapchat Revenue and Usage Statistics (2019)," Business of Apps, August 8, 2017, https://www.businessofapps.com/data/snapchat-statistics.

7. Ani Petrosyan, "Age Distribution of Internet Users Worldwide 2021," Statista, February 23, 2023, https://www.statista.com/statistics/272365/age-distribution-of-internet-users-worldwide.

8. Youth here will mean those under thirteen years of age. As we shall see, it is the most popular demarcation mark for measurement.

9. Though the "internet" was born as early as 1983, the World Wide Web went public for general use in 1993. David Grossman, "On This Day 25 Years Ago, the Web Became Public Domain," *Popular Mechanics*, April 30, 2018, https://www.popularmechanics.com/culture/web/a20104417/www-public-domain.

10. Why lawmakers believed a thirteen-year-old was fully capable of understanding the concepts and risks of data mining, privacy, and exploitation remains shrouded in the mists of time.

11. Tony Newton, "Confusing COPPA Terms on YouTube Lead to More Questions for the FTC," Scalefluence.com, February 6, 2020, https://www.scalefluence.com/confusing-coppa-terms-on-youtube.

12. As a test, the authors went to a couple of sites and tried to open accounts giving our birth year as eleven years before the current date. All denied access. However, when a second attempt was done with the same email and other information, except that the year of birth was made to be one hundred years ago or whatever was the site's maximum year listed, the sites gleefully allowed account creation. Some sites did freeze for about twelve hours, so we just waited, watching some YouTube videos where no age was asked.

13. This is in no way a criticism of school policies, either in their shutting down, switching to online education, or other measures taken in response to the COVID pandemic. We are merely analyzing the impact of such measures on children's online use.

14. Those born since 2010.

15. Ofcom home page, accessed December 14, 2018, https://www.ofcom.org.uk.

16. Martin Armstrong, "Kids on Social Media," Statista, April 6, 2022, https://www.statista.com/chart/27200/kids-on-social-media-uk-survey.

17. Ofcom, "A Third of Children Have False Social Media Age of 18+," October 11, 2022, https://www.ofcom.org.uk/news-centre/2022/a-third-of-children-have-false-social-media-age-of-18.

18. Another impediment to determining underage computer usage is that most surveys of minors often go through the parents. Being third parties, they may not be aware of what their child does or are not forthright in admitting to allowing their child to be online.

19. Kristen Rogers, "Children under 10 Are Using Social Media. Parents Can Help Them Stay Safe Online," CNN, October 18, 2021, https://www.cnn.com/2021/10/18/health/children-social-media-apps-use-poll-wellness/index.html.

20. Rideout, V., A. Peebles, S. Mann, and M. B. Robb, *The Common Sense Census: Media Use by Tweens and Teens, 2021* (San Francisco: Common Sense, 2022), https://www.commonsensemedia.org/sites/default/files/research/report/8-18-census-integrated-report-final-web_0.pdf.

21. Common Sense, "The Common Sense Census: Media Use by Tweens and Teens, 2021," https://www.commonsensemedia.org/sites/default/files/research/report/2022-infographic-8-18-census-web-final-release_0.pdf.

22. Includes websites, social media, and streaming videos.

23. Children from lower-income households also rely more than children from higher-income households on mobile devices such as smartphones for internet access, rather than computers. National Center for Education Statistics, "Children's Internet Access at Home," May 2021, https://nces.ed.gov/programs/coe/indicator/cch/home-internet-access.

24. Microsoft on the Issues, "How Old Is Too Young to Go Online?" October 14, 2013, https://blogs.microsoft.com/on-the-issues/2013/10/14/how-old-is-too-young-to-go-online.

25. Although the term *finsta* was originally created specifically in reference to Instagram, it is now generally applied to any nonpublic social media account on any

platform. It is confusing because the finsta—the *fake* Instagram account—is actually set as a private account and is the one where the kid shows their true activities. The account the parent sees, with edited and curated photos and comments, is called the *rinsta*, or real and public Instagram account.

26. This is not to condemn all finsta/rinsta duplicity. In a very public world, creating dual accounts is a way for youth to maintain a bit of both control and privacy in their lives and communications. They can vent, gossip, and otherwise be kids. It also allows youth to explore and discuss issues they are not yet ready to share with their parents and the world, such as issues relating to identity.

27. Strangely, a 2022 survey of parents as to what was an appropriate age for children to have their own social media account saw the most popular response as age sixteen, with other responses clustered at or above age twelve. S. Dixon, "Age U.S. Parents Believe Is Appropriate for Kids Social Media Use 2022," Statista, August 15, 2022, https://www.statista.com/statistics/1326635/appropriate-age-for-kids-own-social-media-account-us.

28. Jemima McEvoy, "Facebook Internal Research Found Instagram Can Be Very Harmful to Young Girls, Report Says," *Forbes*, September 14, 2021, https://www.forbes.com/sites/jemimamcevoy/2021/09/14/facebook-internal-research-found-instagram-can-be-very-harmful-to-young-girls-report-says.

29. With YouTube dominating.

30. These overlap, as many kids say they watch videos on social media such as TikTok.

31. S. Dixon, "U.S. Young Users Daily Media Activities during the COVID-19 Pandemic 2021, by Age," Statista, January 10, 2022, https://www.statista.com/statistics/1281555/us-kids-teens-daily-activities-coronavirus-by-age. Sadly, Common Sense Media found that actual reading was one activity that did not increase for children during the COVID lockdown.

32. Kelly Burch, "How Does Social Media Affect Teenagers? Understanding the Mental Health Impact—and Why It's Not All Bad," Insider, May 16, 2022, https://www.insider.com/guides/health/mental-health/how-does-social-media-affect-teenagers.

33. A good example is Instagram's 2021 statement with the bold headline "Continuing to Make Instagram Safer for the Youngest Members of Our Community." In it, Instagram, owned as of this writing by Facebook/Meta, says that they require users to be thirteen years old at a minimum but that "verifying people's age online is complex and something many in our industry are grappling with." They then say they are working on it before focusing the rest of the statement on teen usage. Nothing more is specified about blocking users under thirteen. Instagram, "Continuing to Make Instagram Safer for the Youngest Members of Our Community," March 17, 2021, https://about.instagram.com/blog/announcements/continuing-to-make-instagram-safer-for-the-youngest-members-of-our-community.

34. When we were giving a presentation about media to parents some years ago, a concerned mother asked for advice as to her daughter's pretending to do homework or going to sleep in her room but then secretly watching TV till late at night. We said that we would never begin to tell a parent what to do or not do in their house, but what worked for us and our two sons was to only have two TV sets in the house, one in the family room and one in our bedroom.

Chapter 2 Accompanying Lessons

LESSON 2A: TREND SETTING

Focus of Exploration

How online data can show change in culture, at least through words. Data analysis for trends.

Intro Questions/Thoughts for Students

How do sociologists measure and track changes in culture? Can small changes over time show a trend, like the slow height growth of a person? How about changes in language use?

Do you think trends that happen IRL echo or show up online? How so?

Activity

Use Google Trends (https://trends.google.com/trends/?geo=US) to look up words to see when a slang word you use first rose to be popular. Is it more than ten years old? If you find a date with a significant jump in usage, try to think about what was happening then and come up with a hypothesis why the word suddenly became more popular then, such as being used by a pop star or in a show.

Follow-Up Questions/Discussions

Google Trends measures usage in Google search terms, so the relationship—*correlation*—to usage in the real world is indirect. People may be just looking up the word because they heard it and want to know what it means, not using it themselves. Still, their hearing it more might be a sign of greater use. Can you think of other indirect ways to use the internet to see what is happening IRL?

Do you think people use similar language online and IRL? Are there words or phrases you use in one but not the other? Do you use text abbreviations like LOL in real life?

Sociologists use internet statistics to get a big picture of how we live. Are there disadvantages or things you cannot see? For example, *drip* and *drips* increased in usage online around 2018. How can we know from the data how much is due to it becoming a slang description for one's clothes and how much because people had plumbing problems? The term *lasso* is more popular in western states. Do they use the actual rope more, or are they bigger fans of the TV show with the character of that name? What other words might be confusing?

Here we are using what happens online as showing what happens IRL. Can it work the other way around? Is there a way to use the data of what happens online to predict what will later happen IRL? What trends have started online and then caught on IRL?

LESSON 2B: STAYING IN YOUR AGE LANE

Focus of Exploration

Age interaction IRL and online

Intro Questions/Thoughts for Students

How many of the people you talk with and listen to IRL are about your age? How many are in an older or younger age-group? How do you know?

Do you think the people you interact with online are the same age as you? Are there the same numbers of older or younger people? How do you know?

Activity

You will need to be attentive to keep track of this. First, spend as much of a day as you can keeping track of the people you either talk with (two-way) or listen/read their messages (one-way). You don't need names, just make a mark for each one. Don't count the same person twice if you interact with them multiple times. Try to estimate their age and make a mark on a score sheet:

- Person under thirteen
- Teenager
- Twentysomething
- Thirty or older
- Not sure

You can either just make a mark for each or write a *1* for one-way—only one person communicated and the other listened or read the message—or *2* for a two-way interaction where both communicated to each other. Importantly, note any "not sure" interactions.

Once you have done that, spend at least an equal amount of time doing the same thing with how you normally interact online. Keep a tally just like you did for interactions IRL. If you watch someone's video or text with them, count each. You can make a new chart or use the same but use a different color to make marks.

Having gathered your data, you can make a pie chart or bar graph to compare the two circumstances, IRL and online. Use different colors for each age-group, or stripes or shades to distinguish one- and two-way communication—however you think is best to show your data.

Follow-Up Questions/Discussions

Gathering data is only the first part of being an investigator. You have to analyze it and then make it so others can see what you found. Graphs and charts are useful for these last two parts. They take the data and make it so you can see differences that might be important. Later, you can make pie charts of other things, like how you spend your allowance.

Do you see any big differences in the age-groups you interact with online and IRL? Any groups you interact with a lot more or less online? How can you account for this?

Was there a big difference in the "not sure" about age between IRL and online? Why do you think that is? What does that tell you about being careful?

When you do find differences, an investigator has to think of the different *variables* or possible causes. If you interact with a different age-group online than you do IRL, it could be caused by who is online or by what you do there. Both could be factors. Which might it be for you?

If you found an age difference between IRL and online, that answers the "What?" question. The follow-up is the "So what?" question. How could it make a difference in, say, getting information or learning about life?

What is the importance of distinguishing one-way and two-way communication? Generally, people have more two-way communication with people their age and more one-way with others. Why do you think that is? Is that true for you?

LESSON 2C: CALL SECURITY!

Focus of Exploration

Online age security

Intro Questions/Thoughts for Students

IRL, you often see places that limit who can go in, like a teachers' lounge. Why do you think access is limited? What is the goal of limiting access?

Some places or events, such as movies, limit access by age. Again, why do they limit access by age? What is the purpose or goal? Do you always agree? When might you ignore an age restriction IRL and go or do something anyway?

Activity

Look for age restrictions online. Check out the minimum age for social apps, games, or other favorite online places. Ask yourself why they are there. What is the goal or purpose? Is there a potential harm you cannot see? To your knowledge, is the age limit enforced, or is there an easy workaround? Discuss the age restrictions with your parents. How do they feel?

Finally, send a letter, note, or comment to the app or site and let them know how you feel about the age restriction. Do you agree or disagree with it? Would you change it? How so?

Follow-Up Questions/Discussions

There is an expression, "It takes a thief to catch a thief." In this case, one might say it takes an underage person to show how good an app's underage security is. How do you feel about helping that way? Do you know a lot of holes in security?

How much are your parents aware of or support online age restrictions? Should they?

Do you feel there is a lot of effort put into enforcement? Is it better to state an age limit and not really enforce it or to just do away with age limits? Should the decision just be left to kids and their parents? Why or why not?

Is there a compromise? How would you feel about letting kids onto some sites, but they must have a parent present? Would that work? Why or why not?

It's not just places that have age limits. You are probably aware of products that you are too young to use. Make a list of products, such as beer or wine, and activities, such as gambling, that adults can use or do but you cannot because of your age. For each, write out things that you already know about the product, such as brand names, or activity, such as how it is played or done.

Ask yourself how you already know what you know about the product or activity if you are too young. Was it through advertising? Did you learn about it IRL or online? Could letting you know about it have been intentionally done so you would look forward to trying it? Is there any harm to you knowing about these things while too young to have or do them? What may you not know about them? Talk about it with your parents.

LESSON 2D: OPEN PRIVACY

Focus of Exploration

Maintaining secret lives online, or at least not totally open ones

Intro Questions/Thoughts for Students

It's natural for kids to want some parts of their lives private or semiprivate. They may want to share some things with friends but not yet with their parents. Have you ever felt that way? Do you feel that way more as you have gotten older?

Online, do you think it's easier or harder to keep things private or at least limited to a few people knowing compared to IRL? Why or why not?

Activity

You and your parents should discuss privacy. What does it mean to each of you? Does it include not just sharing what you do, but also how you feel and what you think? Does it include doing things unsupervised, like hanging out with friends or chatting online? Discuss the good and bad possibilities of keeping things private. Then, you and your parents should work out a timetable of acquired privacy. Perhaps create a middle ground where you can do it on your own but with parents "checking in" or asking for an update.

You can then make a list of activities with each age that you can do either semiprivately (with parents checking in) or privately (child will tell parents when they need to). You might want to list special conditions that may call for a change, like if the child's grades fall a lot or the parents think the child is in danger. When everyone is happy with the list, everyone can sign it as a pledge to go by it.

Follow-Up Questions/Discussions

This kind of agreement is a contract. A contract is a good device because it helps everyone know exactly what is being agreed upon and the terms. Putting it somewhere where everyone can see it can be a reminder of what everyone promised. If there is a disagreement later about what was said, everyone can look at the contract together.

Even with contracts, there are always emergencies and special occasions that people didn't think about. When such times arise, what do you think is the best way to handle it?

Contracts are good when there are a lot of details or people don't know each other. After a while, however, people develop trust in each other and there is no need for a formal contract. There are understood, unsaid conditions everyone assumes. What are some unspoken terms you and your parents have? What about with your friends?

LESSON 2E: CHARTING A LIFE OF PIE TO RAISE THE BAR

Focus of Exploration

Being aware of how one allocates one's time

Intro Questions/Thoughts for Students

Do you consciously divide your time into categories, like things you need to do versus want to do, or do you just take things as they come?

Are there things that often end up taking too much of your day, or something you wish you could try to do more of? How can you adjust that time balance to accomplish these goals?

Activity

We described in a prior exploratory how to use a pie or bar chart to compare two things. Now here is another way to use them. For an entire day, keep track of how you spend your time. Divide the time into categories such as school, sports, outdoors, time with friends, gaming, on social apps, time with family, and sleep (you can adjust and create categories to suit your schedule). Importantly, "doing nothing" should also be a category. Try to pick a typical day or do this over three or four days and then take the average.

Make a chart of your time, and then study it. Maybe get feedback from friends and family. What categories do you want to give more time to? Which activities would you like to give less time to? Is there another activity you want to squeeze in? Perhaps, instead of doing less of something to make room, you can figure out a way to be more efficient, such as packing your school bag the night before so you can sleep in a bit longer!

After you make the changes, wait a month and then redo this to see if you like it. Like an analyst at a company, you can write a report on the best use of the limited resource of time.

Follow-Up Questions/Discussions

Just like getting healthier is best done slowly and by all-around lifestyle changes, not just what you eat, the same is true for changing how you spend time. Any small change is a step forward. Still, are there any other changes you can do in support of the small change to keep going in the right direction?

We did this for your whole day, but what about if you just did a chart of your time online? Is it trickier because you mindlessly wander to new tasks so it is hard to keep track?

We think of engineers as people who build things. They also build systems. An industrial engineer is someone who creates or refines systems to be better or more efficient. It can be as simple as putting the things you use most often closest to you on your desk. Can you be your own (or the family's) industrial engineer?

We said to include "doing nothing" as a category of your day. Doctors say that doing nothing is an important and healthy part of the day. Why do you think that is?

LESSON 2F: THE COST OF OPPORTUNITY

Focus of Exploration

Opportunity cost

Intro Questions/Thoughts for Students

Have you ever been torn between doing two things you wanted to do? When you eventually choose one thing, do you still think about what you are missing by not doing the other, or do you just think about the activity you chose?

Have you ever had to choose between something IRL, like a sport, or doing something online, like texting or gaming? Do you generally choose real life or being online mostly?

Activity

For a given free afternoon or weekend day, think of a choice between doing something online and doing something IRL. They don't have to be the same activity, just a choice of which to spend time doing.

For each, rate on a scale of 1 (not much) to 10 (a lot) how much immediate enjoyment you would get from the time-competing activities. Then, rate the long-term benefit that will come from doing each. For example, studying may not have high immediate enjoyment, but it will make later preparation easier and free up time to have fun later on. On the other hand, rest and relaxation now can let one recharge to do things with better effort later. You need to total the present and long-term benefits of each to decide which is a better investment of time.

For example, studying might have low immediate enjoyment (2) but a high long-term benefit (10) for a total benefit of 12. Watching a movie has a high immediate benefit (8) but a low long-term benefit (2) for a total of 10. Thus, studying has the slightly higher total and is the better choice!

Follow-Up Questions/Discussions

It's very hard to measure long-term benefits. We don't know what will happen in the future. Because of that, we often just focus on immediate benefits. Is that a good strategy? Why or why not? Can we use past experience to appreciate long-term benefits more?

Rather than making the choice either/or, can we rephrase it to "How much of each?" Then we can maybe split time to get a little bit of both. If so, is it better to do the more fun activity first or second? How can we help to switch, such as using a timer?

LESSON 2G: BUDDY SYSTEM

Focus of Exploration

Buddy system for bad choices

Intro Questions/Thoughts for Students

Have you ever used the buddy system where people keep an eye out and watch each other for safety? Maybe you did it while swimming or hiking. Why is that a common practice? What is the advantage? Can the buddy system be used in other circumstances?

Activity

With your family or class, list five good rules that should apply to everyone about using social media or being online generally. Make a poster of them, perhaps like how swimming pools post their rules. The rules can be about time spent, priorities (like homework first), or behavior (like not being mean).

Importantly, you will all sign your name at the bottom, not to just abide by the rules, but to look out for each other and warn each other if you see someone heading to danger as they venture into possibly dangerous places or activities with social media or being online.

Finally, try to agree to a signal or word that stands out to get someone's attention when you see a potential danger, such as "yellow light" or making a T with your hands to signal a time-out. It should be something that isn't used regularly so it stands out as a warning.

Follow-Up Questions/Discussions

Some warnings are to make a person stop right away; others are warnings to be careful. Should you have both kinds of warnings for being online? For which kinds of activities?

It's hard sometimes to stop right away when another person gives a warning. How can you best agree when you want to keep going a little bit more, but the other person thinks you should stop right away?

Some people start misusing the warnings, such as a joke or too early. What is the danger in doing that? How can that be avoided?

A lot of what we do online is not in front of other people's eyes. How can we help keep our buddies safe online if we don't always see what they are doing at that time? Are there clues we can look for?

Chapter Three

Nudges and Sways in the Online World

The Atlantic must have looked vast and daunting to the first explorers to cross it. It seemed a chaotic mass of swirls, changing winds, and raging storms that came out of nowhere and then disappeared.[1]

Successive explorers, however, shared their observations and slowly, over time, found currents that consistently flowed east and west at certain latitudes and trade winds that blew in particular directions. By the 1700s, maps of the sea lanes allowed venturers to travel with natural forces rather than against them. Ponce de León noted a warm "river" within the ocean in his 1513 visit to Florida, and Ben Franklin charted de León's river in more detail in the 1770s. By the 1800s, that river within the ocean had been identified as the Gulf Stream and the study of it, along with other aspects of the oceans, coalesced into the new science of oceanography.

Today, the internet seems like a vast, mostly uncharted ocean to new users. Online currents can be helpful if they lead explorers in the right direction, such as finding a good discussion thread of information to answer a question. They can also slow progress with a lot of distracting pushes that can take one off course. At its worst, the internet can be dangerous. As they said of the unknown seas, "Here there be monsters."

In this chapter, we will lay out some of the large, general currents that flow through the internet.[2] The current streams can be useful to get online travelers to interesting, fun, and exciting places. They can also be daunting if the venturer is going against the current. The internal flows are both good and bad, helpful and harmful.

See **Lesson 3A: Look Both Ways before Crossing**.

DISTRACTION

Perhaps the strongest force in all of the online world is the sheer force of having so many people, all the time, from everywhere, ready to communicate and connect. People you would never know even existed are a fingertip away from meeting over a shared interest, evolving into a lifelong friendship, and maybe even one day becoming a partner for life.[3]

We wouldn't be doing our lifeguarding jobs, however, if we didn't point out some potential dangers of the great tidal wave of people coming at you through the screen. First, it can be distracting. Most of us have had a moment of almost insight interrupted by an intruding event, a person speaking, or just the "ding" of getting a new message. We then return, only to be lost in a "Where was I?" fog. To have a clear picture in one's mind, one has to have the right frame of mind to put around the picture!

In a story that predates the internet by some 2,500 years, Odysseus and his fellow shipmates, trying to get home after the Trojan War, landed on an island where some of the men were given lotuses to eat.[4] When the sailors ate, they became blissfully forgetful of their wanting to go home, their families, or anything else that mattered in their lives. They had to be forcibly dragged back to the ship until the effects wore off.

Odysseus dragging his lethargic men back to the ship will resonate with many parents trying to get their kids away from distractions to do homework. Most of these activities, such as watching a show or playing a game, are harmless diversions if done in moderation. They are even beneficial in bringing relaxation and fun to people's lives.[5]

Unfortunately, some people are not able to engage in such diversion in moderation and can fall too far behind or even fall prey to addiction.[6] Young minds that have not yet created systems and tools for self-regulation can be especially vulnerable, including being in the always available, always something to do online world or in using social apps.

See **Lesson 3B: B&R—Burst and Reward**.

BELIEVING CURATED LIVES TELL THE WHOLE STORY

Another potentially troublesome current online is feeling bad about ourselves and our own life when we compare ourselves to others online. We should be open to seeing how others do things—it gives us ideas about alternatives and possibilities. We should also be able to share in and cheer other people's success and comfort them when they struggle. Most posters, however, **curate** their lives. They tend to mainly, or exclusively, post pictures and videos when they are at their best. They show the adventure. They capture when they look their best, the one breathtaking shot from tens of them taken.

Unfortunately, many people have said that looking at how great "everyone else" looks and lives makes them feel bad about themselves and their own situation.[7] Studies are now exploring and verifying this common reaction to being inundated with so many upward comparisons.[8] Particularly vulnerable are preteens and early adolescents, who are going through the tumultuous and unsure time of entering puberty. They are anxious about the changes to their bodies, with that anxiety magnified by the amygdala's hijacking of the brain and the emotional responses of puberty's onset. Preteen girls have been found to be particularly susceptible to coming away from social media messaging with a negative self-image.[9]

Most of us know that the internet is not an accurate cross section of how people are IRL. People more often post on social media when they have something positive to share. Many will post a pic of the great meal they had. Few will post a picture of the same boring thing they eat many days, or even that their stomach was upset.

In that sense, social media is one big **sampling error**. Even if we know this, however, we can't help but be affected by the bombardment of images. We compare the boring documentary that is our lives to the sensationalized highlight reel of others'. It's like a world of sways that say, "You aren't doing it right."

See **Lesson 3C: Sample Sizes**.

It's hard to remember this when all we see are pictures of people doing great things, traveling on exotic adventures, and always with perfect hair and clothes. We sometimes feel bad because, let's face it, we seem so ordinary in comparison. We don't stop to ask who wakes up with their hair and makeup done; we just feel bad for not looking like that.

It's like comparing oneself to a fictional superhero in a movie, lamenting that we don't have the same powers, so we must be "losers." The images on social media are edited and curated to be just as fictional, yet they are presented to us in a wave of false reality.

See **Lesson 3D: Curation Creation**.

Again, everyone understands this rationally, but we humans are not always rational. Our self-doubts ask, "Where did I go wrong?" Tweens are trying to sort the world into some sort of order or hierarchy. Unfortunately, the internet seemingly puts ordinary youth in the lower categories and at the back of the line by whatever measure used. It's a tough thing to counter-steer that bad feeling at any age, but tweens have an especially hard time because they are just learning how to master their own thoughts and feelings.

See **Lesson 3E: Ally Up**.

SITES PROMOTE BAD NEWS

While your friends and acquaintances are posting on social media all the great things happening in their lives, the national posters, platforms, and sites often go the other way, dumping a heavy dose of bad news on readers. Why? Think about when two people meet and one asks the other, "How are you?" If the respondent says "Fine" or "Well," the inquirer quickly moves on. If the respondent, however, says they are not doing well or even badly, the inquirer will usually ask why.

We tend to move on from OK or even good news, but dwell on and investigate bad news. Maybe it's our concern for others. Maybe bad news is just more interesting, or we want to see if we can help or if things turn out OK in the end. Whatever the reason, bad news keeps attention. It's hard to think of any fictional story where everything went well and yet the story remained interesting.

Posters on the internet, from huge media corporations to the individual texter, want our eyeballs on what they have to say. So, the bias is to report bad news. It can be so much that often the news won't just report the bad that did happen, but what *could* happen. Another tactic is to ask scary questions in headlines—Is the world ending tonight?—to get you to stop and read the fact that it isn't further down.

Even light celebrity news plays into it. Rarely do the gossip magazines report that the latest pop band is all good, but instead ask if there is drama or a possible breakup looming in their future. The fans worry, so they read on.

See **Lesson 3F: Could Needless Worry Destroy the World Tonight?**

This phenomenon tends to impact adults more as they monitor the internet for issues concerning politics, war, and other strife. **Doom scrolling** occurs when we keep reading more and more bad news, scrolling down our feed to either find something positive or try to see how bad things really are. Either way, the effect of doom scrolling can be almost hypnotic, and leads to generally negative and depressed feelings as we are hit by the tidal wave of bad news. Kids are also vulnerable to being affected by negative news. They do reports on topical events, and news events involving children, from a child trapped in a well to mass shootings at schools, can cause trauma from just hearing about it secondhand.

Children cannot, and perhaps should not, be sheltered from all the bad news. Developmentally, children may not have the emotional tools to understand or process bad news.[10] Kids need assistance in how to hear such stories, ask questions, and, with the guidance of adults, process the information as best they can.

See **Lesson 3G: Dr. Doom Scroll**.

POPULAR OPINION ONLINE IS LARGE, BUT NOT ALWAYS RIGHT

The biggest current of the internet, one might call it the Gulf Stream of it,[11] is the sheer force of crowdsourced popular opinion. Physics teaches that force is derived from mass times acceleration. Online, a single point of view can have both the mass of thousands repeating it and the acceleration brought by electronic sharing. And that's before it is checked as accurate or not.

Humans, despite our individuality, are tribal. We want to be our own person but still comfortably surrounded by others, especially others who think like us. This feeling is especially strong in tweens and early adolescents who are finding independence from their families but looking to form new "tribes" with their peers.

People can't help but be influenced by what looks online like the seemingly "concerted opinion" as to what is the right thing to believe or do. For tweens newly seeking out answers to life's questions, it would almost seem illogical for them to challenge or question what appears supported by so many.

See **Lesson 3H: A Side of Asides**.

Even if a person disagrees, is it worth it to fight the great wave of popular opinion? One risks being separated or losing connection with the group, even in an indirect way. Disagree with a teammate on something outside of the game, and it might affect your relationship in the game itself. Some people might even use people's fear of standing apart from the crowd as a way to pressure a person to act. It doesn't matter if the crowd is wrong—the weight of their view makes the outlier seem like the problem.

This is even more so when the crowd's view is a long-held one, called a tradition. For people who want to be different than what society has said they should be, the weight of today's crowd is magnified by all the crowds of the past, telling the person who wants to explore an alternative that they are wrong, perhaps even immoral. Many social conventions are based on long-held views that are deeply ingrained in society. Examples include gender roles, gender norms, and other stereotypes.

Because these views are often communicated both on a personal level from generation to generation and in a broad sense by media, it is difficult for people who feel like they don't fit into society's pre-molds of identity to have the strength to stand up to the pressure to conform. Even if they have sympathetic and supportive allies on a personal level, they can face the crushing wave of internet opinion from folks who don't know the person or their circumstances, but still judge and label what is different as presumptively bad.[12]

See **Lesson 3I: Going against the Current** and **Lesson 3J: Gender Norms and Normas**.

Related to the fear of being excluded for going against popular opinion is a person's fear of missing out, or **FOMO**.[13] If everyone is doing, enjoying, or seeing something in a particular way, why aren't we? Will our lives be less because we didn't grab or otherwise enjoy an activity "everyone" seems to be doing? The internet can show us new ideas of how to have fun from others, but if we don't find that enjoyable, does it mean there is something wrong with us?

See **Lesson 3K: Fear of Missing Out Is Trending Right Now . . . Don't Miss It!**

THE COST OF BEING ONLINE

For many, a most surprising current of navigating online[14] is the cost. The internet is easily accessed, and there seems to be no ticket-taker at the gate. Most people who jump online don't think about possible costs, just the benefits to be had. Like utilities, such as water or electricity, the internet and social media just seems to magically be there whenever we need it. Stores and other businesses offer free Wi-Fi. Of course, parents and other cost-bearers can explain to youth that, in fact, such things do cost and that we are charged for usage, whether by the amount of data, by a block of time, or both.

What is the cost of using the internet, beyond the money to access it? First is time. As we have said, youth today live in two worlds, online and in real life. For much they overlap, but like trying to stay deeply attentive in a person-to-person conversation while texting gossip on an app, one will eventually block out the other.

The internet wants your time like a store wants your money. Sites often get paid by the time people spend on them.[15] The more time people spend there, the more likely they are to recommend the site to others and to come back. With so many websites and apps to choose from, and the speed with which users move from site to site, sites try to hook and grab eyeballs with **clickbait**, using **eye candy** and other techniques of showing **pop**.

Once they have you, even for a moment, they try to keep you. Web pages invite you to stay engaged by scrolling down continuously with no page breaks to interrupt the flow or, alternatively, by adding "and then . . ." long stories, quizzes, or lists to keep you clicking the "next" button.

See **Lesson 3L: I Want Candy**.

Kids are especially vulnerable to overspending time online. Youth are not experienced in having to weigh and allocate time. They also have a lot more free time, so much that they are often bored and in search of entertainment.[16] Like a billionaire with dollars, kids' excessive wealth of time makes it of less value, so they are willing to spend more of it on frivolous things.

Time is also an abstract idea that exists in large blocks for kids more than in discrete minutes or tied to particular tasks.[17] So, one block of time, such as chilling online, can easily bleed over into the next block, even if the next block is more important, such as homework.

When kids—and many adults—do factor time, they often only think about the event itself and overlook ancillary time-consuming tasks. It's like thinking one has just enough time for a thirty-minute run but not thinking about the time beforehand to get dressed or the time afterward to cool down, stretch, and shower.

See **Lesson 3M: Some Additional Charges**.

Finally, and we really do mean our final point of this chapter, another hidden cost of being online is the giving away of one's privacy. Sites want your data. Many sites get money by offering users something free, such as a game or quiz, but then extracting as much personal information as they legally can. They then sell that data to companies that analyze the data in aggregate for purposes such as advertising. When the internet first began, many users were leery of having their personal data extracted. It felt like being spied on.

Subsequent generations have grown up with the idea that one sacrifices privacy as a cost of doing the internet, so it does not bother them. Youth also feel, perhaps rightly so, that as a typical twelve-year-old, they are not hurt that much by giving away something so abstract as their personal information. COPPA makes it illegal to gather data on underage users, though when an underage user falsifies their age on a website their information can be extracted. It's a hard sell to have youth understand or care about data extraction, though it doesn't hurt to make them aware.

See **Lesson 3N: That's How the Crumbled Cookie Is Rebuilt** and **Lesson 3O: See the Sites!**

NOTES

1. Both **nudges** and **sways,** used in the chapter title, are terms of art. The former was popularized by Nobel laureate Richard Thaler, the latter by us. Both terms are included in the glossary, but a far deeper exploration of the concepts is in our companion book, *Behavioral Economics: A Guide for Youth in Making Choices.*
2. We'll get to more particular aspects starting in the next chapter.
3. Just after the turn of the millennium, the authors here met through what was then a brand-new internet experience, an online dating site. Though many people back then thought meeting a love interest online was sketchy, for us, meeting through our computers was love at first byte.
4. Due to translation, no one is sure if Homer meant the same plant that we today call a lotus.
5. Every new diversion elicits people wringing their hands about how the new frivolity will ruin society. The game of billiards was banned in England at one time for fear of its distracting and corrupting power. Its grandchild, the game of pool, was accused in the musical *The Music Man* of "bringing trouble to River City."
6. New disorders related to the internet are being defined, such as problematic Instagram use, a non-substance-related disorder by which detrimental effects occur as a result of preoccupation and compulsion to excessively engage in social media platforms despite negative consequences.
7. Jay Hill, "How Social Media Is Making You Feel Bad about Yourself Every Day," LifeHack, June 12, 2017, https://www.lifehack.org/600150/how-social-media-fuels-jealousy.
8. An upward comparison is when a person compares themself with someone they perceive as doing better in life or who appears happier. In contrast is a downward comparison looking at someone perceived as doing worse in life or is not as happy.
9. Marika Tiggemann and Amy Slater, "NetTweens: The Internet and Body Image Concerns in Preteenage Girls," *The Journal of Early Adolescence* 34, no. 5 (September 5, 2013): 606–20, https://doi.org/10.1177/0272431613501083. See also Benjamin Johnson, "Look Up, Look Down: Articulating Inputs and Outputs of Social Media Social Comparison," *Journal of Communication Technology* 4, no. 1 (2021), https://doi.org/10.51548/joctec-2021-003.
10. When the attack occurred on September 11, 2001, we withheld immediately telling our own children the details that day, as we had relatives working at the Pentagon and wanted to make sure they were safe. Unfortunately, at soccer practice that afternoon for our six-year-old, one of the other boys kept imitating an airplane flying into a building, making huge explosion sounds and falling down while talking about the "cool pictures" he saw.
11. If one is prone to overextending metaphors.

12. On the other hand, one of the benefits of the internet is for those who feel alone because they feel different, finding support from others like them or allies across the world.

13. Social nudges such as FOMO preceded the internet and are addressed in our previous book, *Middle Schoolers, Meet Media Literacy.* It's a great resource that many educators, parents, and *everyone* else have been using for years, so you shouldn't miss out!

14. And we're sure, to many people's delight, will be the final use of the currents-of-the-internet metaphor.

15. Or they can charge advertisers more if they have higher traffic to their site.

16. The British Psychological Society found that boredom proneness is higher in those under twenty-five than those over. The extent to which this is due to youth needing more brain stimulus prior to the full development of the prefrontal cortex or that society provides more than enough stimulus once people are adults remains unknown. Unfortunately, boredom proneness returns for the elderly. James Danckert and John D. Eastwood, "Boredom across the Lifespan," British Psychological Society," June 8, 2020, https://www.bps.org.uk/psychologist/boredom-across-lifespan.

17. Even with adults, the more abstract something is, the more it is spent. Adults will spend more with a credit card than paying with cash.

Chapter 3 Accompanying Lessons

LESSON 3A: LOOK BOTH WAYS BEFORE CROSSING

Focus of Exploration

Awareness when navigating the internet

Intro Questions/Thoughts for Students

You were probably told to "look both ways" when crossing a street. What was the message of that phrase? How can it apply to other potentially dangerous situations?

Activity

Make a list of potentially dangerous places or circumstances, even safe places that nevertheless may have hidden dangers. For each, write out the dangers at that particular place. Also write out the good that can come from being in that space or using it, even temporarily. Finally, write how the advice to "look both ways" applies to each place or circumstance.

Now, do the same thing but for places and circumstances you find online, from chatting on social media to gaming and any others, applying the "look both ways" advice. What do you need to look out for?

Follow-Up Questions/Discussions

If the "look both ways" advice does not really apply, are there other safety sayings, like about talking with strangers, that might apply?

Sometimes places seem safe or so familiar we drop our guard and stop looking out for potential hazards. How can you avoid being lured into a false sense of safety? What reminders can you put around you to stay on guard?

Even when we know there are dangers, we can become a "deer in headlights," transfixed and not going to safety even as we see the danger coming. How can you make sure you keep "moving" to safety when a threat or danger shows itself? Can you use a buddy system?

Between the danger spots are safe grounds, like crosswalks and medians with streets. They are not absolutely safe, but they offer a place to catch our breath and be a little more at ease. Where are such spaces for you online? See if you can find an online group that discusses or is centered upon an activity, hobby, or passion of yours, a group you feel an **affinity** with.

If you feel comfortable doing so, add a post or share something safe, like a picture of your pet to a cat lovers group. One big advantage of the online world is that a person might be embarrassed to share their personal passion locally but happy to do it with more-remote people online.

LESSON 3B: B&R—BURST AND REWARD

Focus of Exploration

Pacing to get through tasks and online

Intro Questions/Thoughts for Students

What does the saying "Keep your eyes on the prize" mean to you? Do you ever imagine a reward ahead of time as a way to keep you focused and going? Does that help?

What are physical sports and activities that require intensive bursts of strength or effort? What do the people who do them do between these bursts? Maybe a tennis player relaxes his or her grip between points, a soccer player stands still for a moment, or a dancer watches other performers?

Activity

Super concentration is like a burst of mental running. It is high intensity but only lasts a short while. Runners and other athletes often break their strenuous efforts into short, intensive bursts that are more effective.

Make a list of something you need to do. It can be physical, like raking leaves, or more mental, like doing homework. Divide the job into parts, maybe doing a quarter at a time.

Also make a list of some things that you like. Maybe checking text messages or getting a snack. Maybe taking a run around the block. Importantly, each one should last no more than five minutes. Put a reference to each one between the sections of the job you have to do, so that you will do a burst of what you need to do and then a quick reward break.

Follow-Up Questions/Discussions

This technique of a productive burst and then a quick reward is a handy tool for schoolwork and later a career. We used it in teaching with grading and even in writing this book!

Burst and reward, or B&R, is also important in being online. Doctors are saying it is not healthy to sit in one place for hours, so building in breaks and movement are good for the body as well as the mind. Hey, it's time for ours right now!

One tricky part of B&R is keeping the reward to five minutes. It helps to set a timer that forces you to get back to it. Another way is to put the more liked rewards later, with an ultimate reward when one is done. Putting one's homework on top of a game console can be a reminder that the ultimate reward comes after all is done.

There are many ways to subdivide the work. You can subdivide by time or by subject. You have to find out what works best for you and your situation. You may find it is easier to do homework for two subjects before taking a break, or you may find it is easier to do an hour of intense work and then take a short break.

Some tasks are better done without a break so the focus is not lost and has to be regained. What kind of tasks might not work well with a B&R strategy?

LESSON 3C: SAMPLE SIZES

Focus of Exploration
Sample size and sampling error

Intro Questions/Thoughts for Students
When you see posts by someone you don't know, whether texts, photos, or videos, do you form ideas about what their whole life is like? How much of a person's life do you need to see before you can make accurate assumptions about what they or their life is like?

Activity
For someone you personally know well, like a friend or a parent, look at their social media posts. If you knew nothing about them except what they posted, what are important things about them or their life that is left out? Do they include all their family? Is their typical day, as far as you know what it is, represented in their posts? If the person showed food or fun activities, did they show all of the activity or things in that category or just the highlights?

Follow-Up Questions/Discussions
If you have an idea, even a rough one, of the amount of time the person typically spends in a day doing different sorts of things (eating, sleeping, working, having fun), compare it to the percentage of posts that show the activities. Were some activities overrepresented? If so, which?

Does the accuracy of the posts to the person's life depend on the purpose of the account? Are posts more for recording their life or showing off / promoting themself to the world?

Is everyone posting to some extent to show off? Is that bad?

We often judge people as happy or sad, having a good or bad time, even being a good or bad person, by very small glimpses into their lives, called a **sample size**, but not knowing the full story. In statistics, this is called a **sampling error** (making a conclusion on not enough data).

Has anyone ever judged you wrongly based on a sampling error? Is there anyone you know that maybe you should get more data about their life?

Do you have a social media presence? Does the sample of your personality or life reflect you accurately? Are you OK with that?

LESSON 3D: CURATION CREATION

Focus of Exploration

Curation

Intro Questions/Thoughts for Students

We often see photos and videos of people's lives, but how much is that representative of their day-to-day life? Do people tend to post what typically happens in their life or just the highlights?

Do you ever feel bad about your life when you see other people's posts?

Activity

For one day, keep a log of what happens in your life as much as possible. Record the food you eat, the time asleep, and if you are bored, working, or having fun. Try to track the time spent doing things. At the same time, take pictures or videos as if you were documenting the day.

Then, lay out the pics or edit the videos as if you were going to post them on social media. Choose which moments you want to show to look good and impress people. You can use an app like Instagram that has a layout preview (but don't actually upload, to keep your privacy), or lay them out on a word processor. Remember, your goal is to impress to get more viewers (and maybe sponsors!).

Follow-Up Questions/Discussions

Did you do any retakes because the first shot wasn't what you liked? Did you purposely redo something to show it in a better way? Did you do anything special to look good, like wear certain clothes or touch up your looks? Why did you do those things?

Would there have been a difference in what you chose to document if you were doing it as a personal diary for others to really know you? How so?

What if your goal was not to impress, but to show how boring your day was (maybe that's why you need something special for your birthday). Could you use the same pics you took and re-lay them out to send that different message?

Social media and internet videos don't show the whole story. The stories are **curated** to show people at their best. Is this OK? Does it depend on how the poster presents the pictures?

Most people know that social media and internet videos are curated, but we often still feel bad in comparison. Why do you think that is? When is curating too much like false bragging? What can we do to not feel bad in comparison to the incomplete, even fake, depiction of others' lives?

Would you prefer people also show the bad times of their day or moments in life when things go wrong? Why or why not? Do you ever feel better about yourself when someone else admits things didn't go well for them either? Do you admire people who show themselves not at their best? Why or why not?

Curating our lives is not new. When we talk with someone and tell them about a past event, we might choose to include some details ("I scored the winning goal") and leave out others ("It was actually a lucky shot where the ball bounced off my foot"). When is it OK to do this, and when may it not be?

LESSON 3E: ALLY UP

Focus of Exploration

Finding help on the internet

Intro Questions/Thoughts for Students

Do you ever have a problem or worry but feel like you don't have anyone to talk with about it? What do you do?

Do you ever find your mood changed after being online? If so, does it more often make you feel better or worse about yourself and your life? Why?

Do you ever go online because you feel bad about yourself or your life? Does it help? What about it makes you feel better? It is more that it positively helps or that it gets your mind off the bad stuff? How long does the good feeling last?

Activity

Sometimes the best way to ask for help online is to be direct. If you are feeling sad or worried about something, try typing it in directly, such as "I am worried about my grades" or "Why do I feel lonely?"

Look at the search results. Some may be links to organizations that help people who feel the way you typed in. Others may be posts from people who feel similar.

Follow-Up Questions/Discussions

If you don't have any major concerns or worries, consider this exercise a drill. You can do this when you do have concerns or bad feelings about yourself or what's going on in your life.

It's almost always better to talk with someone who knows you and cares about you. If not someone who knows you well, seek out a professional near you, like a school counselor. Still, we don't always have that available. If you go looking on the internet, it's very important to remember there are good and bad advisers online, people who know and people who don't. There are also people looking for youth and others with problems they can exploit. It's risky. A well-established organization is better than an unknown individual who may or may not have your best interest at heart. What should you look for in seeking advice? What kind of information should you be careful of giving away online?

Even in trusting what seems like good people or organizations, some organizations are better than others. Some people are sympathetic, some will just coldly say "get over it." The advantage of searching like this is seeing what connections and resources might be out there, especially if you have no one IRL to talk with. Don't just jump into the first sites returned. Do some further digging and, if possible, get advice from parents, counselors, or trusted friends, if not about the problem, then where to go for help.

Sometimes going online isn't a cure for what troubles us. It is an escape for our mind. When is this OK to do? When might it not be good to do?

LESSON 3F: COULD NEEDLESS WORRY DESTROY THE WORLD TONIGHT?

Focus of Exploration

The internet making people anxious through speculative language

Intro Questions/Thoughts for Students

Could the world end tonight? It's very unlikely. More likely is that you, because of that question, are now thinking about the world ending. Have you ever been nudged to start thinking about things just because someone asks a question? Did that question do it?

Activity

Read news on the internet about current events, pop stars, anything you wish. Look for when such stories, which are supposed to be giving you information, instead seem to ask questions. You can find questions faster by searching [ctrl+F] for "?". When you find them, look at where the questions are—headline, top of story, in the middle—and whether they actually ask a question you had or bring up a new thought. Is the question open-ended ("What's going on with . . .?") or suggestive ("Could it be that . . .?" "Is it true that . . .?"). Are the questions more about positive or negative things?

Follow-Up Questions/Discussions

Were there a lot of questions in the headlines? Were the questions in the headlines directly answered in the article, or did the article go in a different direction? Headlines are supposed to *tell* you about the story. Why then are there questions in them?

Were the questions about specific sensational things—big breakup or news—or about everyday things? Did they seem to lead you to topics? Are we doing the same thing with our questions here?

We think of questions as a device to get information. How else can they be used? A question can also be used to introduce a new topic. Another way to use questions is to guide or direct a discussion by making it seem like the person communicating is answering a question the audience has but is really talking about what they want to discuss, like the second sentence in this paragraph.

How can you tell when a person is answering questions you or others might have or is just trying to introduce a new topic or to **nudge** or **sway** you into thinking about what they have to say? When is it OK to nudge or sway people by asking questions?

Why would people intentionally try to make you worried by a "Could it be . . .?" question? Deep down in our brains is a part that jumps us into "fight or flight" mode when we see or hear about danger. It takes control of us, even overriding the logical parts of our brain that caution "Wait a minute!" Could some of the anxiety questions be tricks to get you upset so you pay attention to them and suspend reason?

The bottom line here is what to do when you read things online that make you anxious. You can keep in mind that questions can nudge or sway you just in the asking. You can also realize that just because a statement, question, or topic is online, it is not "published" or even fact-checked. What else can you think about or do when you read news that makes you anxious?

LESSON 3G: DR. DOOM SCROLL

Focus of Exploration
Internet effect of bad news

Intro Questions/Thoughts for Students
Does reading news online make you generally feel more positive or negative? Why? Does it depend on the kind of news? If so, what kinds or topics make you feel better? What kinds make you feel worse?

Activity
"News" just means the delivery of information about recent or important events. It is not supposed to be more positive or negative, just what is happening. To test that, spend a day on a news site looking at articles. For each, mark if it reports generally good news that's inspiring, bad news that makes you worried or concerned, or is neutral. You can make a pie chart to show your results. To minimize the risk of **sample error,** try to repeat the investigation on different days of the week and compare percentages of good and bad news.

Follow-Up Questions/Discussions
Was the news more positive, more negative, or neutral? Is it what you expected? Do you think the balance of good and bad news is more a reflection of what is happening or what the sites choose to report? How can you check? In deciding, you may not think you know enough about the issues to judge—either the tone of the article or the way the world is. Still, your perspective is important too, as well as the way you feel in reaction to the news.

Did you find the tone of headlines accurately reflected the good news / bad news tone of the articles? Did you find yourself more drawn into headlines that were positive, negative, or neutral? Why?

If you did the activity for a couple of weeks, do some days seem to have more good or bad news than others? Why do you think that is?

If you did it with others, were there any articles where someone thought it was positive news and someone else thought it negative or neutral? Why is that? What does that tell you about interpreting news?

Would the balance of good and bad news be different if you examined sports or entertainment? If it is different, why do you think that is?

Most importantly, when you read news and begin to feel bad, what can you do? Can you look for good news? Is it better to turn away for a little bit? How can you make yourself do that?

LESSON 3H: A SIDE OF ASIDES

Focus of Exploration

Influencing opinion by subtle nudges and sways

Intro Questions/Thoughts for Students

Have you ever watched a video about one topic but then come away thinking about another topic, maybe something casually brought up by the person?

Do you believe someone more if they are forceful and direct, saying you must believe it, or casual and say it in an "everyone knows" way? Does it matter if the person is a friend?

Activity

Look up a bit of news that has more than one side to the issue. It can be about politics, sports, fashion, entertainment, or anything else. Now record a two-to-three-minute video of yourself talking about another topic as if you were going to post it online on social media. As you speak, casually work in your opinion on the issue you initially looked up. Don't make it too forced, but mention it as an aside.

Ask others to watch your video. Afterward, ask them if they picked up any other information or opinions on anything beyond the main topic. Even better, have a partner make a video that makes an aside on the same first topic but from a different viewpoint. See if people pick up the difference.

Follow-Up Questions/Discussions

Do you think asides can **nudge** or **sway** people into having a certain opinion or point of view? What about a lot of asides from lots of people all saying the same thing?

How can you tell when you hear something said several times if it is true, the whole story, or an opinion shared by people outside your circle? When should you look into an opinion more before accepting it?

The internet gives us a lot of opinions. It can also seem like the same opinion is shared by lots of people, even if it isn't. It can be an **echo chamber** where one opinion bounces around. How can you be on guard or double check if something "everyone says" is actually said by everyone?

LESSON 3I: GOING AGAINST THE CURRENT

Focus of Exploration

Disagreements online

Intro Questions/Thoughts for Students

When people disagree, do you think they are more polite face-to-face or online? If you see a difference in how polite or respectful people are, why do you think that is?

Have you ever seen where two people disagree and then others join in? If you have seen it both in the real world and online, do the people joining in seem more polite or rude IRL or online? Do the joiners act the same IRL and online?

Have you seen a person who has a different view, opinion, or lifestyle driven out of a space or even a community simply because they have disagreed with the majority? What about online?

Activity

Look for places where strangers disagree online. Also look for circumstances where the people disagreeing know each other or have some established relationship, such as IRL or in a social media group. Compare the disagreement when people don't know each other, such as in the comments section of a news article. Compare the tone.

Next, look at situations where those commenting are roughly evenly divided, or at least there are numerous people on either side. Compare that to when it seems like there is just one person or a few advocating something different to a larger group. Do you see a difference in tone?

Follow-Up Questions/Discussions

There are two variables here, whether the disagreement is IRL or online and also whether the people know each other or don't. For the know or don't know each other, does one case happen more IRL and the other more online? How can you control one variable and remove it as a factor?

When we get caught up in a disagreement, or even just come up against something different, sometimes our deep-seated "fight" impulse arises. Can you tell the difference between those disagreeing on the issue and those attacking the people with different views? When you read people insulting others, does that make you more inclined to side with them or not? Why?

Was there a difference in tone when people argued with a group that was large versus arguing against just a few or even one person with a different view? Was there any ganging up? Why do you think that can happen? Do you think people ever hide their disagreement for fear of having a mob come at them? Is that good for the group as a whole? Why or why not?

We think of a "mob" of people ganging up as happening IRL and have certainly seen it. Can it happen online by people who aren't even together physically? How? If you are in a large group that seems to be ganging up on a single person or a few, what can you do to tone down the group or get them to remember to be respectful?

What are ways to "lightly" disagree to state your view while minimizing bad feelings? Some people use the sandwich approach where they give a compliment or agree with something said ("I can see why you would say that"), then state why they disagree ("On the other hand . . ."), and then finish by positively looking for common ground ("Can we agree it's not 100 percent one or the other?"). Do you think this technique works? When might it not?

How can you leave room for differences of opinion and still maintain a community, especially online? We may disagree on opinions, but how can we remember we are still dealing with people and that they should be treated as you would want to be treated?

LESSON 3J: GENDER NORMS AND NORMAS

Focus of Exploration

Gender norms online

Intro Questions/Thoughts for Students

Do you think there is a difference between what boys do online and what girls do online? What are the differences? How did you come to that belief?

How do you think boys and girls are represented online in terms of what they like to do? Do you see a difference? Is it accurate for you and your friends?

Were you ever told that "Boys do . . ." and "Girls do . . ."? Do you think telling people that affects what they in turn choose to do?

Activity

Look online at as many activities as you can. Also check out topics of chat in social media and in discussion forums. Divide the activities and topics into those that seem to have more female participants, more male participants, or are about equally mixed (as best you can tell).

For whatever gender you identify with, see if your activity and topic preferences are the same as the general trends you see.

Follow-Up Questions/Discussions

If you found gender distinctions, do they mirror what happens IRL? Are they more or less so?

Did your preferences seem to be similar to those of a lot of your gender? It's hard to tell, but how did you come to like or prefer that activity? Did you pick it on your own, or did people suggest it to you? Is that like or preference equally suggested to all genders as far as you can tell, or to one more than others? Why or why not?

If you could tell, how are people treated whose gender is different from the majority who shared an interest? Were they welcomed as equals? Was there any discussion or references made about gender? If you have a preference or interest in something generally not shared with your gender, do you feel embarrassed expressing your preference or interest? Why or why not?

Do you think there is pressure for people to be interested in particular activities or topics because of their gender? Where does that pressure come from? Have you ever felt it? If there was pressure to participate in something because of your gender that you really weren't interested in, what could you do? What if you saw someone harassed or left out because of their gender identity? What could you do?

LESSON 3K: FEAR OF MISSING OUT IS TRENDING RIGHT NOW ... DON'T MISS IT!

Focus of Exploration

Changing popularity and trending on internet, FOMO, bandwagon effect

Intro Questions/Thoughts for Students

Do you remember what was popular on the internet six months ago? A year ago? It could be a site, a game, a person, or even a word or phrase.

What does **trending** mean to you? Perhaps ask several people what they conjure in their mind.

Activity

Do an online search for "What is hot?" or "What is trending?" for things like fashion, music, or food (or whatever you wish). You may have to do searches with different words (*hot* and *trending*). You can also see if there is a difference if you add *internet* or *online*. Use **Boolean operators**, which are connectors like "hot *or* trending." You can even put phrases in parentheses like an algebra problem, such as "What is trending *and* (internet *or* online)."

When you search, take advantage of the fact that most search engines allow you to time-limit your search. For example, you can click on "Tools," then click where it pops up "Any time." There, you can choose "Custom" and enter a range so you can just get results now or from six months ago, one year ago, or five years ago.

Follow-Up Questions/Discussions

How many of the past trends do you remember? How popular was the trend? Can you tell if the trend lasted or how soon it died out? Is it still around today?

For whatever trends you see are going on now, were you aware of them? If you weren't aware of a current hot trend, does knowing it's a trend make you want to check it out or even try it just because it's popular? Is that a good enough reason?

For the past trends, did you miss any? If you did, do you regret not knowing about them? Imagine if there were a hot trend your friends knew about and were doing, but you didn't know about it. How would you feel? Would you feel bad, even if your life was fine, except for not knowing about the trend? This is called **FOMO**, or fear of missing out. It's that uneasy feeling that many people are participating in a hot trend but you are not. Have you ever had FOMO?

If people are motivated to try or buy something because of FOMO, might other people try to push their product or self, nudging consumers by claiming "Everyone loves it" or "Don't miss out"? Can you find online and IRL where people say that?

Have you ever been tempted to do something because everyone else was doing it? It's called the **bandwagon effect**, from the old idea that a big wagon comes down the main street of a town, playing loud music, and everyone wants to jump on board. Have you seen where people hear a "noise" of a trend and rush to jump on it? When is joining the crowd or wanting to keep it together enough to be a good reason to join in? When should people think about it before they join in?

If you are unsure or feel that doing what everyone else is doing is not right for you, what strategies can you use to politely not do it? Will your friends and others respect that decision? Would you respect others who don't join in doing what you like?

LESSON 3L: I WANT CANDY

Focus of Exploration

Distractions, clickbait, eye candy

Intro Questions/Thoughts for Students

When you are scrolling through text or on sites, what grabs your attention? Is it particular colors or activities? Certain words or people?

What kind of pictures make you stop and look? A particular kind of man or woman? A particular scene or activity?

Does your stop-to-look impulse change depending on what you are doing online, such as homework research, video-watching, chatting, or gaming? How so? Are there things or people that grab your attention no matter what?

Activity

For sites you regularly go to, start at the top and then scroll down at a fast, but not extreme, rate. If something makes you pause, think about what it is and why it made you pause. Make a note of the kinds of things that make you pause your scrolling and look:

- Exciting headline
- Celebrity picture
- Picture of a good-looking or interesting person
- Picture of something you like (cats, sport, etc.)
- Animation
- Reference to something you like (gaming, fashion)
- Something else (describe)

Look for commonalities or patterns of what makes you stop and drop (eyeballs).

Follow-Up Questions/Discussions

When something grabs your quick attention, it is called **eye candy**. To be eye candy, it must have **pop**, loosely described as the "Whoa!" factor. Based on your scrolling, what kinds of eye candy have the most pop for you?

Eye candy, like real candy, is fine and fun so long as we don't mistake it for real nutrition (like when candy tries to say it's healthy!). The same goes for information. Did you find any eye candy that you first thought was good information but then realized it was for fun or to just grab you rather than lasting information?

Is there any danger to being too distracted by eye candy too often? When driving a car, we can't help but look at interesting things, but you know you are supposed to keep your eyes on the road. Is driving around online the same thing? When you have to work online, such as research for school, how do you keep from being distracted by eye candy?

Distractions can also occur even as we are looking at what we need to. Studies show that no matter how much we think we can multitask, we can't focus on multiple things well and we can lose important details, even if we get most of it. A famous test of this is called the Stroop effect.[1] You can do a similar test for being online. Pick out a Wikipedia article to read. While reading it, open another window with a flashy video (or play your favorite song). Afterward, have someone quiz you on the Wiki article to see how much of the detail you got.

How do we stop being distracted? The famous Greek hero Odysseus knew he and his men were about to sail by the Sirens, creatures who sang a beautiful song that lured men on ships to steer their boats to rocks and sink. Before they got there, Odysseus had his men fill their ears with wax so they could not hear the Sirens.

As for himself, Odysseus, also known as Ulysses, ordered that he be tied to the mast so that he could hear but do nothing. Binding yourself for a future event no matter what happens is called a *Ulysses pact.* Think of something you need or want to do but has distraction risks, like needing to read homework but you might get distracted by text messaging coming in. Can you bind yourself by putting things out of reach? How can you commit yourself so you will not give in to temptation?

Distractions can also be countered with a buddy system. We often don't realize our mind is drifting, but if we are doing something with a partner, they can nudge us if we seem to drift. Also, knowing they are relying on us can give us extra motivation. What is an activity where you can bind yourself with a buddy to not be distracted?

---

1. Try taking the Stroop test at https://itservices.cas.unt.edu/~tam/SelfTests/StroopEffects.html.

LESSON 3M: SOME ADDITIONAL CHARGES

Focus of Exploration

Hidden costs on being online

Intro Questions/Thoughts for Students

Have you ever gone to buy something thinking you knew the price, but then ended up paying more? What were the extra charges, like tax? Once you were aware of the extra charges, why did you buy it anyway?

Have you ever gone to buy something and then discovered afterward that you paid more than you should have? How did you feel? Was the item purchased still worth it?

When you figure the cost of buying something, do you just look at the price it sells for? What are "hidden" costs, like the cost of the gas to get there or the electricity to buy online? These costs are small, but they are costs and can add up. What are other ones?

When you think about the cost of something, do you think about the cost in time that you have to spend?

Activity

Find a time tracker on your search browser (Google has one) and install the app. These monitor your time usage while online, both in total time and as to individual sites.

Now play around online for thirty minutes. Go anywhere you want, but don't look at any clocks or timers. Cover the clock or hide the toolbar while you do this. Just rely on your own sense of when thirty minutes has gone by.

Afterward, compare how well you did guessing the time with what the web tracker says. If you also estimated how long you were on each site, compare those amounts as well.

Follow-Up Questions/Discussions

Once we decide to buy something in real life, we often are so committed that when we are hit with extra surprise costs, we pay them because we don't want to back out. Is that the same as with time being online? Is there ever a point where the surprise extra costs of money or time are just too much?

Your estimation here was while consciously being aware of a time experiment. If you weren't doing an experiment, do you think your estimate would be the same? Keep the web tracker installed and then, after a week, compare your estimate of how much time you were online to what the web tracker says. As a percentage, were you better or worse at estimating for the longer period? Why do you think that is?

Do you think your "overpaying" of time online is more without realizing it or more a conscious "just a little bit more" decision that adds up? What are good strategies for avoiding both kinds of overpayment of time?

Just like there are hidden monetary costs to buying something, there are hidden time costs to being online. Do the exploratory again but log how much time it takes you from the moment you decide to get online until the time you are on it. After being online, log any time spent afterward to transition to the next activity, such as putting away anything.

LESSON 3N: THAT'S HOW THE CRUMBLED COOKIE IS REBUILT

Focus of Exploration

Computer cookies

Intro Questions/Thoughts for Students

If you were in a store and a security guard followed you around watching and recording what you did, would it bother you? What if the store said they did it to better serve you?

What if the store security guard kept following you after you left the store? What if the store, again, said they did it to better know who you are and what you liked to better serve you?

Activity

Cookies are text files or markers placed by websites on computers when you visit them to identify you for when you return and, in some cases, to continuously track what you do online so that your usage data can be collected. Let's see what's in your computer.

On your browser, look up how to clear the cookies or small trackers on your computer.[1] After a week of being online as you normally would, look at the cookies that are on your computer. Again, you can look up how.[2] Look at cookies for sites you visited. Also look for cookies for sites you did not visit. How do you think they got there?

Follow-Up Questions/Discussions

Does the tracking by sites you visit bother you? Why or why not? How can collecting your data possibly help or harm you? What about the sites you did not visit? They bought the "right" to also place cookies.

Sites that put cookies on your devices do their best to keep the information private, but they can be hacked for their data on you and the information stolen. In fact, someone hacking your computer can take the cookies and impersonate you. Does this potential risk bother you, even if it is relatively small?

Most sites explain their cookie policy in the "terms and conditions" posted on the site. Have you ever read it? Do you think most people read the terms and conditions even if they click "I agree"? Why or why not?

You can not only clear cookies, but also adjust your browser to not allow cookies or to allow only certain ones. Try it and see how far you can get before a site demands you allow its cookies to visit it. Is that demand OK in your opinion? Is it like a store saying you must agree to their terms to enter?

In Europe, people are allowed more choices to opt out of cookies when they visit a site. There are exceptions, such as for "necessary" cookies, and one has to take more time to just get into a site. What do you think of that option? Is it too much of a bother, or would you feel better visiting sites?

Big shopping sites use cookies to see your shopping patterns, even searches, to then try to sell you things the **algorithm** calculates you might like. Create a new account on a shopping site like Amazon. While signed in there, look for crazy or silly things to buy. Sign off and then after a couple of days sign back in. What are the reminders of what you were looking at? Same or even related products?

The store's keeping track of what you shopped for in private makes it possible for the information to become public. Someone logging into your computer could see it. Someone hacking into your computer, or the online store's site, could get it. What kind of things could you be shopping for that you don't want to keep a record of?

1. For example, on Chrome click on the three dots at the top right corner > More tools > Clear browsing data > Clear data (make sure "Cookies and other site data" is checked).

2. Again for Chrome, click on the three dots at the top right corner > Settings > Privacy and security > Cookies and other site data > See all cookies and site data.

LESSON 3O: SEE THE SITES!

Focus of Exploration

Gamification of dangers online

Intro Questions/Thoughts for Students

The Odyssey is one of the oldest stories still around today. It is about Odysseus and his men sailing the Aegean Sea to get home and all the challenges and dangers they faced. There are other sagas about going on trips or voyages, such as Gilgamesh or the Ramayana. They are all stories of people on a quest who must travel far and face dangers. They must use their wits and abilities to get out of traps and reach their goal. What stories do you know that are like that?

Why do we all like stories that are like travel sagas and adventure in facing dangers?

Activity

We have been exploring in this book, at least on paper, the currents and traps that carry us about in traveling online. Now let's put some together as a saga.

List all the possible traps and boons (good things) that can come from being on the internet. Then, create a board game that uses them. The game can be around the board or a swirling, meandering quest. Put in spots where travelers encounter traps and have to suffer consequences from them, such as wasting time (losing a turn) or having to do silly things. You can put in good things that happen, like finding the perfect information that leads to a shortcut. You are the designer of this internet saga, so you get to make it how you wish! Be sure to decorate it, perhaps with pictures you get online!

Follow-Up Questions/Discussions

Like making anything, you may find glitches and problems as you test-play your game (called *beta testing*). Get feedback and revise the game to make it better. It's what every good inventor does.

The hardest part is often writing out the instructions for your game so that anyone can play it even if you are not around to explain it.

If you think your game is really good, you can submit it to a game publisher or magazine. Where can you find them? Online, of course!

Chapter Four

Stubborn Things (Fact-Checking Online)

In the fall of 1770, Boston was an occupied city. The citizens of Boston were agitating against British government oppression and intrusion on their rights. The British government, in response, was sending more and more soldiers to suppress dissent.

In the midst of this begins a trial watched not only by almost every Bostonian but throughout the colonies as they teeter on the brink of making a united demand for independence. Eight British soldiers stand trial for murder. On March 5 of that year, a crowd of angry colonials that formed against British taxation and oppression confronted a group of British soldiers. While some facts remain disputed and lost in time, we know that church bells rang to incite more people to join the angry crowd. The colonials had no guns, like the British soldiers did, but they had shovels and clubs, along with assorted pieces of wood and ice chunks. The crowd pressed in and threw objects at the soldiers.

A piece of wood struck one soldier, and he then fired his gun. Whether it was an accident, a gut reaction, or intentional is, again, lost in the chaos of the moment. Other soldiers, however, also began to fire. The captain tried to order the soldiers to cease firing, but his voice was lost in the confusion. By the time it was over, five colonials would die, and the British soldiers would surrender and then be tried for murder.

For the colonials, there was no need to wait for a court to pronounce the soldiers guilty. Within a month of the shooting, silversmith and engraver Paul Revere would circulate a depiction of what was then being called the "Bloody Massacre," today remembered as the Boston Massacre.[1]

The soldiers had difficulty finding lawyers who would represent them. People had already decided their guilt, and attorneys were afraid of the negative publicity of representing the men. Finally, three attorneys took the cases, including a prominent Boston lawyer, John Adams.

Adams was unquestionably a colonial patriot who opposed British tyranny and would come to support independence and lead the colonies to it. He would be part of the group of five that would write the Declaration of Independence. Still, Adams was in favor of legal justice for everyone, whether colonial merchant or British soldier.

Knowing public sentiment as the trial came about, Adams stuck with a simple request of the jury: Put aside your passions and stick with the facts. In what has come to be one of Adams's most famous quotes, he told the jury: "Facts are stubborn things; and whatever may be our wishes, our inclinations, or the dictates of our passions, they cannot alter the state of facts and evidence."[2]

If you are wondering what any of this has to do with the internet, take a look at just about any big issue online that has grabbed public attention. You will find multiple and contradictory information and opinions cross-fired. Predecided judgments on the issue proliferate similar to how Boston citizens cried "Guilty!" before the soldiers' trial. The idea that one is innocent until proven guilty is lost in calls for summary judgment and swift punishment. People attack not only counterarguments but those who make them, **poisoning the well** to discredit them.

See **Lesson 4A: Only an Idiot Would Not See the Poisoned Well**.

The wonder of the internet is that we no longer have to run to the library to research a question; we can do so from our home.[3] Unfortunately, the information comes in like a power hose shoots water. What's more, the water is a mix of filtered and unfiltered, clean and tainted.

Adams's advice that we must stick with facts and not let other things like our passions and desires taint our views remains sound. Even with potential access to more information as we have today online, two problems remain. First, people jump to conclusions before they have all the facts. They often cherry-pick information, looking for confirmation rather than information.

Second, there is a basic misunderstanding of the difference between a "fact," an objective statement describing what is, and an "opinion," which is an evaluation or conclusion using facts . . . hopefully. A ball thrown by anyone will act in certain ways as the laws of physics demand. Those are facts. Whether the ball will be thrown well and hit the target is up to how the person threw it. That's opinion.

See **Lesson 4B: F or O?**

The internet makes no distinction between accurate and inaccurate facts. It broadcasts them all. One can find "facts" asserted by both sides that cannot coexist at the same time. Conclusions based on inaccurate or incomplete facts stand next to those by people who have done thorough research. Online opinions are not boosted by accuracy so much as sensationalism or popularity. A nearly three-hundred-year-old truism, variously attributed to many people, is that a lie can travel halfway around the world while the truth is still putting on its shoes.[4] In today's internet world, a lie can go **viral** and travel before the truth even gets out of bed.

The task of fact-finding and evaluation is tough on the internet for anyone, but even tougher for youth. They don't have experience that says, "Wait a minute . . ." to dubious facts. They have been told to trust authority, or at least those who claim to have **authoritative** knowledge.

Looking for information and answers online, the deluge of contrasting information makes us resort to shortcuts, or **heuristics**, to figure out what to believe. Such beliefs can help, but they can also trip us up when misapplied. The British government was oppressive and violated colonial rights in 1770, but that did not mean every act by every British soldier warranted conviction. Even opinions held by everyone are still opinions, not facts.

As we said in the last chapter, we humans are tribal. We take our cues from others. When we want to know if a statement is factual and should be believed, we look to popular opinion through techniques such as **crowdsourcing**. Many times, that's helpful. In real life, the collective shout to not go somewhere can save a person's wallet or even life. Online, heeding a hundred negative reviews of a restaurant can save our stomachs.

Of course, the shortcut of going with public opinion can also lead to trouble if we are not careful. The crowd, no matter how big or loud, may not be right. Consider a hypothetical young student assigned to do a science report back in 1692 Salem on witches. The intrepid student looks for information on *ye olde* internet, and, well, you can guess the "facts" she found, just prior to her own arrest for witchery for consorting with a magic box powered by lightning!

See **Lesson 4C: "Everyone knows . . ."**

Part of what fuels crowdsourcing error is the **bandwagon effect**, which says that for many the gravitational force of a crowd's behavior, customs, and even beliefs is too hard to resist. If it's **trending**, it must be right. The internet can be a hot spot for band-wagoning, from fun challenges[5] to everyone liking or disliking someone in the news. Over time, many people go from "How can I not miss out?" on a trend to "What were we all thinking?"

Another problem with crowdsourcing facts is knowing if the crowd is indeed a crowd or just a loud minority. One might have ninety-nine scientists who are saying one thing in their academic circles and are too busy researching to make internet comments. Meanwhile, the one who disagrees is loudly and sensationally proclaiming to the world what only he personally believes as "common knowledge."[6]

Before we leave the heuristic of going with popular opinion, it's worth it to mention the opposite people, the rebels. They are the people who push back, even reject something simply because the crowd likes it. They proudly declare they are not sheep and refuse popular points of view. But are they being truly independent? If they reject what is popular, then they are as much influenced by popularity as those that follow the crowd.[7]

Some people look skeptically on things that suddenly become popular. They believe the newly popular cannot be of the same quality as the time-tested. For years, the *New York Times'* Best Seller list was a leading influencer on what people chose to read. Of late, however, people have consulted alternatives such as the hashtag #BookTok, where posters make recommendations of books they enjoyed and say why. People are finding the hashtag helpful, as they can get recommendations directly from people who seem to have the same taste in reading.

Which is the best heuristic, then—to go with the crowd or to reject popularity as a relevant factor? For any question, there are persuasive opinions and arguments, especially if the responses appeal to answers the researcher had in mind as they began to search. How can they determine if the opinion is sound, based on good and sufficient evidence? How can they tell if what they're getting is based on **misinformation** or even **disinformation**?

See **Lesson 4D: Re-Bias**.

Researchers have to decide if the source, whether a single person, an organization, or a crowd, is authoritative: Is it a source that can be trusted as knowledgeable about the subject?[8]

There are some clues we can look at to see if a source is authoritative. One way to have authority is to have firsthand knowledge of an event or circumstance, having been there when it happened. Such eyewitness testimony can't give a person the entire, big picture, but they can describe in detail one particular aspect, or even speak to a general feel of the situation.

On the other hand, any eyewitness testimony brings to that observation all their preformed opinions to the observation. The person may have not been paying full attention or had something blocking part of their vision. They may think red sports cars always drive recklessly or have some other **bias** that filters what they observe.

See **Lesson 4E: Secondhand Goods**.

Another way that a source speaks with authority on a matter is if they are an expert, having experience, knowledge, or training greater than the average person. This is often reflected by their having **credentials**, such as degrees, training, experience, or other assets that allow them to have more understanding of the topic or issue.

Of course, a credentialed expert may have their own biases, and not all experts will agree. One should also see if the supposed expert source has high regard in their field among peers or overseeing organizations. Still, expert opinions are worth considering, especially if one is trying to get a big picture of the entire issue, especially complicated ones.

See **Lesson 4F: Who's Talking to Me?**

When evaluating a source for authority, there are some things that may seem to make the source more believable but are actually red flags to be wary of. When a source says theirs is the only source to be trusted, that they are 100 percent certain, or that the answer is simple, one should be a bit skeptical. Most issues that one has to research are complicated. If many people have different perspectives on it, that should be a warning that the issue is not so "simple" or even "clear."

Something psychologists have found is the **Dunning-Kruger effect**, whereby people with lower skill or expertise tend to overestimate their ability and knowledge relative to others. Having not explored all sides themselves, they claim that they know all and that their view is the only legitimate one.

On the other hand, people who really study an issue or topic will tell you that questions usually lead to more questions. Experts are more likely to answer a question with "It depends" because they have seen so many cases where a simple rule does not always apply. In looking for answers, we are often drawn to the quick, definite answer, but an investigator looking for a more accurate answer needs to be patient and put up with ambiguity sometimes.

See **Lesson 4G: Eye-Brain Tag Team**.

A second ambiguous credential for authority is listening to experts in a field outside the topic. A researcher might hear that the provider of information is a doctor, but are they the right kind of doctor for this topic? There are medical doctors, PhDs, and still other kinds as well.

Even within the medical field, there are many different specialties, where a doctor might be very knowledgeable about one area but not know a lot about another. The same is true for most every profession, from attorneys to engineers. A researcher must be careful to see what is the area of specialty that the expert is knowledgeable in and that the topic is within that area.

A common error in deciding authority is to confuse what has been authoritatively published with what is merely made for public viewing. In the case of the former, fellow experts review and critique opinions, called **peer-reviewed**, before it is published. Sometimes scholarly articles lie in academic corners of the internet, such as journals, not visited by the general public. In contrast, anyone can put something, true or untrue, on the internet. It may look authoritatively published, especially if it appears on a popular site or social media platform, but it may or may not have been double-checked.

The law currently exempts internet sites and platforms from responsibility for what others post on their site as long as they do not endorse or claim to verify it.[9] Because of the law, online platforms and sites will state that they do not double-check the accuracy of things posted. Some sites will say they do mark or even remove posts that they find to be inaccurate, but that doesn't mean that what is posted has been determined as accurate. The site might not have gotten to it yet. A 2022 study found that more and more users were getting news from TikTok.[10] Unfortunately, TikTok has a poor record of catching disinformation on their site.[11] To be fair, TikTok was not intended at its inception to be a news source.

See **Lesson 4H: Reliable Sources Tell Me . . .**

A final trap we can fall into regarding authority is a big one. Ironically, it's a trap we create for ourselves. We want to feel we are right about things even before we look into them. So, when we judge information as to whether it "sounds right," we give the nod to any information that we believed before we ever started looking. This is called **confirmation bias**.

While confirmation bias comes from inside us, the internet can give us back our own opinion but make it look like it's coming from somewhere else. It's called the **echo chamber**. Back in 2011, Upworthy cofounder Eli Pariser discussed what he called **filter bubbles**.[12] We may share information and our opinion with a friend. What we shared is then passed to another friend, and another, till it circles back to us. We read it and think, "Huzzah! I was right as confirmed by this other party!"[13]

Social media looks like a vast network where we are in touch with everyone on it, but in actuality it's more like small, bubbled communities where the same information is passed and repassed. Apparently, no one is immune to falling for the echo chamber, not even the US government.[14]

Another cause of the echo chamber effect is the result of **algorithms**. We hear the term used a lot and it sounds complicated, but it is simply the rules that programmers put into a program to tell it what to do. Algorithms can be as simple as commanding that a value less than 0.5 be rounded to 0 and that 0.5 to 0.999 be rounded to 1. It can also order search results in a certain way.

Knowing that people like to feel smart and reinforced, algorithms for most sites like to feed you back or at least prioritize what it thinks you already like or are familiar with. If you are researching dogs and then go online shopping, the site's algorithm, seeing your interest in dogs, may suggest some canine-related products whether you have a dog or not. Similar algorithms will look at your history of shopping and suggest related products, like an easel for the person who buys art supplies.

Algorithms act similarly when researching for information. Two people can research the same topic, such as Spain. The search engine will return sites that discuss traveling in Spain for the person who has previously looked into vacations. For the sports fan, the same search engine might suggest *fútbol* sites. We think search engines are neutral, but they give us back what they—or their designers—think we want based on our own prior actions. Even something as simple as a texting algorithm with auto-suggest tries to give us back what it thinks we want, sometimes to hilarious mistakes.

See **Lesson 4I: Autofrantic**.

The internet promises answers instantaneously. Internet service providers measure their performance in speed, even down to milliseconds. That creates in us an expectation that answers should be immediate. We look for the quickest, most at-hand answer to our queries.

When we ask a question, search engines will give us more sites than we care to look at. Search engines like Google even offer suggested questions based on yours, a sort of "What you may be asking is . . .," to then give you answers. All these suggestions are not only gathered but ranked, by the search engine's algorithm. The algorithms, including all their rules of how they rank search results, remain the secret of the company.

It takes time, but a good researcher needs to look at several sites and not just the first ones listed. It might be on point, even the best site for that information, or it might be what the algorithm thinks you *want* to see.

Some companies try to game the system by using tricks to get their site listed higher, including working in common search terms on their site or even paying for being listed higher. You might see a small designation that it is a "sponsored site," "ad," or other hint. Paying sites may not give you unbiased information but rather information to immediately nudge you, or to long-term sway you, into buying what they are selling. They can even be a rip-off.[15]

For example, searching for where to buy tickets for an event such as a concert or sports event, the first result might be a secondary market that offers resale tickets that paid to be the top search result.[16] Mindlessly taking the first result can be as unhealthy as walking into a convenience store hungry and grabbing the first thing one sees without checking out what it actually is. It can make a person GAG when they grab and go like that.

See **Lesson 4J: Does a Chrome Firefox Go "Bing" When It Goes on Safari with a DuckDuck?; Lesson 4K: What's My Algorithm?;** and **Lesson 4L: Your Googleganger Is Showing!**

We discussed in the last chapter how many sites try to have **pop**. Pop is not just used for entertainment, it's also used in delivering news and information. Clickbait headlines grab your attention. The more sensational the headline, however, often the more the article says something different.

More common of late is delivering opinion masquerading as information in a short, clever statement or entertaining picture, made to be passed around and shared. These are better known as **memes.** Memes are great. They make us laugh. They give us a shared culture or phrase we can all be a part of. They can inspire us to be better, like to be kind or to volunteer.

What memes cannot do is provide in-depth information or understanding of a topic or issue. They tend to reduce a topic, event, or even a person to a single point, often exaggerated for humor like a caricature. When memes are about a controversial issue, the makers and reposters tend to reduce counterarguments, and even the people making those counterarguments, to oversimplified or exaggerated objects that are easy to knock down, called a **straw man fallacy**.

Memes hit us emotionally, and they should not be confused with appealing to our rational parts. They play on our confirmation bias as we shout, "That's right!" How long have memes been around in America? At least since Paul Revere did that illustration back in 1770.

See **Lesson 4M: Meme's the Word**.

Another danger to be aware of when you search for information online is **hedging**. Advertisers love to use hedging strategies when they are unsure or can't say something is 100 percent. The keywords to look for are *mostly*, *probably*, or *nearly*. We can be so fast to read and get an answer, we miss the hedge and report the facts as *always* and *100 percent*.

Take, for example, "There's solid evidence that whole grain oats and oat bran can help lower blood cholesterol thanks to the power of beta-glucan—a soluble fiber, largely unique to oats, that basically tells your liver to pull LDL cholesterol out of the blood."[17] So, does eating oats reduce bad cholesterol? Well, that depends on what "solid," "evidence" (is that the same as a medical study?), and "can help" mean. Can you get the same benefit elsewhere? That depends on what "largely unique" means.[18] Still, asking people will elicit a memory that they have heard that oatmeal reduces bad cholesterol. No hedges or buts.

We cannot say outright[19] that advertisers and other users of hedging are doing so to deceive. They are a varied lot. We, however, the digesters of information, must be on guard. Declarers of absolutes, such as "All X people are crooked," will retreat to hedging when asked if that's really true, from "Well, almost all," to "Many," to "I met one once." It also helps, when confronting hedging or an absolutist, to simply ask for the source and support for their declaration.

See **Lesson 4N: Maybe Baby**.

Hedging uses indirect messaging, hoping that the message receiver, in a hurry, does the heavy lifting and fills in what the messenger wants to be communicated. Another method is called **innuendo**. That is when something is implied, but never actually stated, and it's usually bad or negative: "I'm not saying they are cutting class. I'm just saying I saw them this morning and they are not here now." They may not be saying, but it's pretty clear what they are saying.[20]

There are other ways to use innuendo. **Rhetorical questions**, which are questions that already suggest the answer, are used to suggest things under the guise of just asking questions.[21] Even without words, the mere placing of things side by side, called **juxtaposition**, sways viewers to associate the two things, especially if the things look similar. If the message receiver is in a hurry, the innuendo can leave them with information that is inaccurate and unproven, but vague enough so the source of innuendo can deny the obvious implication.

See **Lesson 4O: Just Sayin'**.

The takeaway from all of this is that the internet is a great assistant for helping us learn, but we should never give over the thinking and judgment aspects of learning to it. We should take information in, but always be asking if the information is good. Preformulated and supplied opinions should be considered but weighed. It's like a real-life detective solving a mystery. Many clues have to be gathered, compared, and waived. Rarely is the path a straight line. Some clues go to dead ends.

As convenient as it is to just accept what information comes our way, we cannot be passive receivers when it is important that we fully understand. We may have to go out of our way to find it. For all the internet gives us, it lacks the most important tool in learning that you have, an active brain to judge if something is worth knowing and using.

NOTES

1. Dave Roos, "How Paul Revere's Engraving of the Boston Massacre Rallied the Patriot Cause," History Channel, August 16, 2021, https://www.history.com/news/paul-revere-engraving-boston-massacre. Revere's illustration became the single greatest propaganda tool for inciting colonial resistance to Britain. It was reprinted for many years, even after the trial, to reignite colonial anger. Today, it is reproduced in almost every American history textbook. Ironically, there remains a question of whether Revere plagiarized the picture from another illustrator.

2. Founders Online, "Adams' Argument for the Defense: 3–4 December 1770," National Archives, n.d., https://founders.archives.gov/documents/Adams/05-03-02-0001-0004-0016. Of the eight accused soldiers, six were found not guilty. Two, who were accused of deliberately firing, were found guilty of manslaughter. No one was found guilty of murder. While the colonists were not happy, the verdicts gained the respect of the international community. They saw that despite the British telling everyone that the colonials were savages, in fact Boston and the rest of the colonies was a place where universal rights and laws would be upheld. Of course, the plight of slaves, women, and other marginalized citizens was another issue. Adams later reflected that had the soldiers been found guilty and executed, it would have likened the colonists to their past mob mentality that executed witches to appease public sentiment.

3. That people no longer need or do go to the library is not necessarily a completely good thing!

4. Quote Investigator, posted July 13, 2014, https://quoteinvestigator.com/2014/07/13/truth.

5. Planking to ice-bucket dumping to Tide Pods, to name a few.

6. Even when there appear to be numbers backing up a view or giving a thumbs-up, it is easy today to buy those thumbs by paying for more positive reviews and ratings. There are **bots** that can do the liking, posting, and raving for a price.

7. One of the authors here had, as part of his signature teen look, his shoelaces not tied. When untied shoes became a fad, he then declared his independence from crowd influence by now always tying his shoes! Rebellion as a guiding sway in making choices is examined in our companion book, *Behavioral Economics: A Guide for Youth in Making Choices*.

8. In the field of rhetoric, this is more formally called an ethos appeal to authority.

9. The famous Section 230 of the Communications Decency Act. As of this book's writing, Section 230 is being reviewed by the Supreme Court and its revision is being debated in Congress.

10. Katerina Eva Matsa, "More Americans Are Getting News on TikTok, Bucking the Trend on Other Social Media Sites," Pew Research Center, October 21, 2022, https://www.pewresearch.org/fact-tank/2022/10/21/more-americans-are-getting-news-on-tiktok-bucking-the-trend-on-other-social-media-sites.

11. Global Witness, "TikTok and Facebook Fail to Detect Election Disinformation in the US, While YouTube Succeeds," October 21, 2022, https://www.globalwitness.org/en/campaigns/digital-threats/tiktok-and-facebook-fail-detect-election-disinfor

mation-us-while-youtube-succeeds. This is not even considering that TikTok's parent organization is in China, making it susceptible to pressure from the Chinese government to filter information on certain issues. Facebook was shown to be slightly better at catching disinformation, while YouTube was shown best of the three tested.

12. Eli Pariser, "Beware Online 'Filter Bubbles,'" TED, March 2011, https://www.ted.com/talks/eli_pariser_beware_online_filter_bubbles?language=en.

13. Yeah, no one really talks like that.

14. Back in 2002, the US government received intelligence from Italian sources that Iraq was trying to acquire uranium for weapons. In fact, that information was based on fraudulent documents, but the United States received a report from Great Britain saying the same thing, seeming to confirm it. Unfortunately, Britain's source for the bad information was the same bad Italian source the US got its information from. In essence, the US got the same bad intelligence information twice from the same source, but it thought it was verified, leading to subsequent bad decisions.

15. An unfortunately common and successful scam are sites that claim to give the telephone number for Facebook and other sites' customer support. Facebook has no such number, but because so many people have searched for one, scam sites have arisen that, when called, try to get money or even control of the caller's computer in the guise of helping them.

16. If one buys a resale ticket from an unofficial—but official-looking—site and then wishes to change seats or pick another event, one cannot do so at the event or with the main ticket seller.

17. Quaker Oats, "Helper of Hearts," 2023, https://www.quakeroats.com/extraordinary-oats/keep-your-heart-healthy.

18. This site is neither the only nor the worst user of hedging, but is a good example.

19. Catch that hedge?

20. A common giveaway of innuendo is that the messenger says "All I'm saying is . . ." and then implies much more than what they are saying.

21. Has no one else explained rhetorical questions as well as we have?

Chapter 4 Accompanying Lessons

LESSON 4A: ONLY AN IDIOT WOULD NOT SEE THE POISONED WELL

Focus of Exploration

Poisoning the well technique

Intro Questions/Thoughts for Students

Have you ever heard an argument or debate in which one side describes everyone who disagrees with them negatively? Have you seen where instead of discussing the issue, they insult the person who believes differently? Does that help convince you?

Activity

Look at debates or even arguments online, such as in chat and in the comments after a news article. Look to see if anyone makes a group description or negative comments about those who disagree with their view. It can be insults, like calling them "unintelligent" or "uninformed." It can also be questioning their motives, saying they are doing it to help themselves. It can even be making them all out to be enemies or at least "not my friends." Think about the group description by the well-poisoner. Does the person have proof of the accusation other than they disagree? Is the proof against one person or everyone?

Follow-Up Questions/Discussions

Sometimes this technique of attacking people who disagree—called **poisoning the well**—is done to stop other people from going over to the "other side" ("If you agree with them, you aren't my friend"). Do you see the tactic used more between friends, say on chat, or between strangers arguing about something?

When someone tries to poison the well by insulting people who disagree, does that convince you more to side with them? Does it ever backfire and make you less likely to agree with them? Why or why not?

Poisoning the well is often a sign someone is taking a discussion too personally or emotionally. How can you stop yourself from getting too emotional in a disagreement? An interesting model are trial attorneys, who often debate each other in court yet try not to take things personally. They have to work together to settle the case. Also, today's opponent may be tomorrow's ally.

Part of the difference between arguing online and IRL is that online the person you disagree with is not directly present. That can make them less "human." It allows a person to then throw out comments without someone stopping them. Do you think poisoning the well, and other **flaming** techniques, is more common online than IRL? Why or why not?

When people discuss, even disagree on, something, the goal should be for them to work together to find a better understanding of the big picture. That often lies between or in a combination of all views. When a person insults different views, it's like they are not seeking understanding but just to "win" the argument. How can you disagree with, even oppose, another view but still seek middle-ground understanding?

Flaming and negativity can be perpetuated by third parties watching a disagreement. Look for reviews or descriptions of people disagreeing where a commentator says one person was *destroyed*, *blown away*, *crushed*, or similar aggressive terms. That makes the discussion sound like a violent sports contest—even after those participants shake hands.

An honest disagreement is by people each trying to find the truth, not to win. "Crushing" someone and making them feel bad and resentful will likely not get them to agree with your view. Still, we find this language used all the time by people describing other people's disagreements, especially online. Why do you think that is? When you are in a disagreement and you feel the disagreement getting too personal, what can you do to take a break or tone the situation down?

LESSON 4B: F OR O?

Focus of Exploration

Fact versus opinion

Intro Questions/Thoughts for Students

What is the difference between a fact and an opinion? What is an example of each? When is it better to use each? How do we use the two together?

Generally, facts are statements based on data or statistics. They do not change from different people's perspectives and can be verified by any other person. That we live on Earth, or your birth date, is a fact. Opinions are based on each person's individual perspective or personal evaluation. Whether something, such as a kind of food or band, is good or not is an opinion.

Be careful because there can be seeming overlap between a fact and an opinion. Saying something is "short" or a band is "popular" looks like an indisputable fact, and most people may agree, but it is still a matter of perspective—what defines "short" or "popular"?—and so is a widely held opinion.

Former US senator Daniel Patrick Moynihan once said, "You are entitled to your opinion. But you are not entitled to your own facts." What do you think he meant by that?

Activity

Find an article on a topic you like. It can be news, entertainment, sports, or something else. Copy the article into a Word or other document. Now go through the article again, highlighting every statement of *fact* in one color, such as pink, and every statement of *opinion* in another color, such as yellow.

Follow-Up Questions/Discussions

Was it hard to tell the difference between fact and opinion sometimes? If you did it with someone else, did they disagree whether something was a fact or an opinion?

When should a news article be based more on facts than opinion? When is it OK to have more opinion than facts? A report of a drought or water shortage in an area? A review of a band's latest musical release?

Sometimes people believe so strongly in their opinion and think there is no way anyone could justifiably disagree, so they say it is a fact. Did you find any of those? Do you have any of those opinions?

We can also get confused about facts because of small differences in language, called *semantics*. One person says, "We live on Earth." Another says, "No, because the atmosphere is part of the Earth system, so we live *in* Earth." This is semantics. Did you find any of these?

If you are trying to discuss something with someone, is it better to start with facts or opinions and work from there? We often disagree in our opinions, but what do we do when we disagree on or use different facts?

LESSON 4C: "EVERYONE KNOWS . . ."

Focus of Exploration

Errors in common knowledge. Using the internet to fact-check.

Intro Questions/Thoughts for Students

Have you ever believed something many others did, only to find out later it wasn't true? How did you learn it wasn't true?

What does it mean when something is "common knowledge"? How does something get to be common knowledge?

Activity

Search online for "famous false facts in history" or a similar search. You can make a collage of all the famous false facts. You can also list two true facts plus one falsehood and ask people, especially your parents, which one they think is false.

Follow-Up Questions/Discussions

How do you think false facts "everyone knows" begin? How do they spread? Do you think the internet helps to stop the spread of false facts or speeds it up?

How much of the spread of false facts happens because we want it to be true or it's interesting? How can we stop ourselves from spreading false facts we like?

More modern or recent popular false facts are called *urban myths* or *urban legends*. There are sites, like Snopes, that research and verify urban myths. Other sites, like PolitiFact, check out claims made in speeches for accuracy. Check out these sites and find some interesting and surprising untruths. Of course, you should ask if these sites, like any you check, are themselves accurate in their investigation and reporting.

When you hear people stating facts you know or think may be false, how can you politely say that? When is it important to speak out, and might it be better to let the false fact slide?

Why do some people hold on to a false fact even if the evidence shows it is not true?

LESSON 4D: RE-BIAS

Focus of Exploration

Detecting bias in reporting. Offsetting biased reporting.

Intro Questions/Thoughts for Students

Have you ever read or heard a report about something, such as an argument or someone's opinion, and thought you were only getting part of the story, like maybe there was another side?

Activity

Think of a situation that might have two (or more) perspectives, such as a political debate or whether a movie is good. For that subject, find two articles that give opposite assessments of it. Copy the articles into Word documents and then highlight facts and examples that only one or the other refers to in different colors, such as blue and pink. If you find facts or examples that are common to both, highlight them in yellow.

Follow-Up Questions/Discussions

Do the two articles have more facts and examples in common or different? Does one, or both, leave out important information that the other includes?

Do you feel like you get the whole picture from one article? Might there even be a third or more perspectives? How can you know when you have learned enough? Can you form an opinion but remain open to changing it if you find out more information?

When someone gives you a one-sided view, it is **biased**. Removing any prejudicial or slanted opinions, or demanding objective proof for assertions, is called *de-biasing* something. Another way to go is what you did here, called **re-biasing**. If bias tilts the perspective one way, adding a different, opposite opinion helps to rebalance the perspective by seeing it from another angle. If all your friends have one view of a situation or person, getting an outsider's view can re-bias the total perspective. What are the benefits and possible dangers from trying to re-bias information about an issue?

LESSON 4E: SECONDHAND GOODS

Focus of Exploration

Difference between firsthand and secondhand reporting of information

Intro Questions/Thoughts for Students

You may have played the telephone game, where one person whispers something to someone and it is passed around until the last person says it aloud. It usually is a different phrase from the original. Why is that? What does that tell you about getting information indirectly?

Activity

Look at news reports of events or review a chat in social media about an incident. Copy and paste the story or chat into a Word document. Highlight witness statements where someone describes what they saw or experienced firsthand in one color and anything reported secondhand, such as saying they "heard," in another color.[1]

Follow-Up Questions/Discussions

Did you find more firsthand or secondhand reporting of what happened in the news stories? What about among friends or in chats describing an event? News stories try to go with firsthand eyewitnesses, but in casual conversation we often go more with second- and even thirdhand ("A friend of a friend told me . . .") reporting. Is that OK?

  In court cases, secondhand testimony is usually not allowed. It's called *hearsay* (as in the witness hears it and says it, like the telephone game) and is considered unreliable. It doesn't have to be just words. Think about if someone told you they were inside but knew it was raining because they saw someone outside with an umbrella up. That's hearsay because the person we really need to ask is the person outside. Maybe they wanted shade from the sun, or it had rained earlier and they forgot to close the umbrella. It can be tricky. Not even lawyers always get hearsay right.

---

1. A third kind of statement you might get, which you can ignore for now, is someone not giving facts or describing something but making conclusions or interpreting what others say happened. They may say what the rules or laws are, or what is generally believed. These are "experts"—though their ability to analyze what others say can be up for debate.

Hearsay is very common in gossip. When you hear someone talking about something they did not actually witness, what can you say to politely make sure what they are saying is correct, or at least say that there may be something else going on?

LESSON 4F: WHO'S TALKING TO ME?

Focus of Exploration

Finding experts online

Intro Questions/Thoughts for Students

When you need expert advice or opinion, where do you go? How do you find experts?

How can you know if someone who claims to be an expert is one?

Activity

You have been assigned to put together a seminar on a favorite topic of yours to your class. It can be on news, politics, music, fashion, or sports; on a specific person, band, or team; or on anything else. Imagine, however, that you must bring in two experts on your topic to speak. Search online for experts on your topic.[1]

There really is no technical definition of an "expert," except that they are more knowledgeable than the general population and, hopefully, their audience. Expertise generally comes one of two ways, from studying the topic thoroughly or from gaining firsthand experience doing or being involved in the topic.

Try to find one expert of each kind. List your two experts, along with their **credentials,** or what makes them an expert. What is their field of study or experience that makes them an expert?

Follow-Up Questions/Discussions

When you were searching for experts, did you start with a site devoted to your topic or search generally for "experts in . . ."? What is the difference between searching each way?

Did you find potential experts but decided not to use them? Why not? What are reasons to not use someone as an expert even if they are knowledgeable? For example, can someone be very knowledgeable but also very biased? Another may have experience or have studied a lot, but not this particular issue.

---

1. Don't worry if you can't really get them to come in, like a famous athlete or scientist!

LESSON 4G: EYE-BRAIN TAG TEAM

Focus of Exploration

Witnesses and experts forming the whole story

Intro Questions/Thoughts for Students

When you want to know what happened in an incident, when is it better to hear from eyewitnesses? When is it better to hear from experts to help you understand what happened or its meaning? If you need to know if the light was red or green when the car went into the intersection, is it better to have an eyewitness or an expert? How about if you want to understand how long it takes for a car to brake to a stop? When do you need both together?

Activity

Find a news story. In the story, identify the eyewitnesses and indicate what they add to your knowledge of the topic. Then identify the experts and identify what they add to your understanding of the topic.

Follow-Up Questions/Discussions

Sometimes the one-two punch of eyewitnesses and experts is summed up by saying the eyewitnesses answer the question "What?" and the experts answer the question "So what?" The first gives us knowledge; the second gives us understanding. How does that apply to the story you found?

For a problem or situation in your life, how would witnesses and experts, together, help you to understand it?

LESSON 4H: RELIABLE SOURCES TELL ME . . .

Focus of Exploration

Source checking

Intro Questions/Thoughts for Students

When you get information from someone or a site, do you ever ask if it is reliable or credible? Are there clues in how to tell if a source is credible?

Activity

Find articles on a topic you like that quote experts or organizations, especially for their opinion. For the site you found the article on, search "How reliable is [name of site]?" Look at other sites that evaluate or give a rating for the site. Is the site known for reliability or is it debatable? Has it been found to have reported things incorrectly in the past? Then search out the expert or organization quoted or cited in the article. Search "How reliable is [expert's or organization's name]?" Do they seem reliable?

Follow-Up Questions/Discussions

When you read news on a site, there are two levels that need checking because a mistake at either level can make the news incorrect. The first is the original source, the person or expert referred to in the article. The second is the site reporting what the first person, their source, says. Reliable news sites have mistakenly quoted fake or bad sources or reported a statement out of context.

Reporters and news organizations are supposed to have policies about **disinformation** and how they guard, identify, and remove disinformation on their sites. Unfortunately, many sites have bad records of either detecting or removing disinformation. What is the record of the site you took your information from? Social media sites have particularly bad records at identifying and removing disinformation. Why do you think that is? What does that tell you about getting information on social media as opposed to a news site?

Sometimes a site that offers news has clues that it should not be trusted. It is always critical of one side of an argument or seems to always talk up one person. The site is run by people who are supporters of someone involved in the story. Look for a site like that and point out the clues.

In the end, it's a lot of work to keep double-checking sites and their sources. Many people therefore find a site or two they judge as reliable and then only get information from that site. What are the advantages and disadvantages of that strategy?

LESSON 4I: AUTOFRANTIC

Focus of Exploration

Accuracy of algorithms to know us

Intro Questions/Thoughts for Students

Have you ever been speaking and someone you know finishes your sentences? Are some people better at knowing what you are going to say, and others less so? Why do you think that is?

Activity

Have a phone in hand that has autocomplete enabled. Text to no one in particular (unless you actually plan to send it) "Yesterday I . . ." or "My favorite thing is . . ." or "For my birthday I want to . . ." Then hit the middle suggestion of autocomplete ten to twenty times.

Read your autocompleted text. Is it accurate for how you would answer it? If you actually send it to a friend, have them send one back and compare the differences and similarities.

Follow-Up Questions/Discussions

Autocomplete uses an **algorithm** to predict what you are going to say next. It is based on what you have texted before as well as what people like you have texted. The big question is, however, is it you or what you would have said?

We think of computers as "smart" but in actuality they can only do what programmers tell them to do (for now). Even their learning is based on rules that are programmed. For autocomplete, the algorithm tends to assume that what you did before is what you want to do now. When might it not be a good rule of prediction? When might it be useful?

If you exchanged texts with a friend and you had differences, where do you think those differences came from in terms of what the algorithm picked up?

Most any computer program, including quizzes online that tell you who "you" are, uses algorithms. How do you feel about trusting them? Can they be a starting point but then one has to also be open to seeing how it is not quite you? In what ways do you consider yourself more "typical"—so that the algorithm can predict your response—and in what ways are you atypical in that the algorithm might be incorrect about you?

LESSON 4J: DOES A CHROME FIREFOX GO "BING" WHEN IT GOES ON SAFARI WITH A DUCKDUCK?

Focus of Exploration

Difference in search engine algorithms

Intro Questions/Thoughts for Students

What is the browser you use most often when searching online? Do you only use that one? Do you use the same browser at home and at school?

Activity

Think of something you wish to purchase, like a game system or tickets to a concert. Or maybe help someone in the family shop for something unusual, like tires for the family car, or plan a vacation. Search for it on your usual browser and copy the first page of the screen results. Then, do the exact same search on at least one different browser, capturing that screen. Compare the results. Are they the same?

Follow-Up Questions/Discussions

If the search results are different, it is because the **algorithms** that tell each browser how to prioritize the results have different rules. Using different browsers is kind of like checking out different libraries. Most of the books and sources are the same, but you might find a real gem in a particular one that the others don't have so available. When might it be worth it to use different browsers to research?

How are the results different for shopping? Are different stores prioritized? Why do you think that is? Some browsers allow companies to pay to get a higher rank. Can you tell which ones paid for that? Look for clues like a site at the top saying "sponsored."

If the results are different for shopping, would the results be the same if you were looking for news or information for school?

Even if your home and school computers use the same browser, you might get slightly different results doing the same search. You can also try doing the same search on a friend's computer with the same browser. If you see differences, it could be based on a number of factors, including what people who have used that computer have searched before or what the computer settings have blocked. Try it and see if you can account for the differences.

LESSON 4K: WHAT'S MY ALGORITHM?

Focus of Exploration

How algorithms work

Intro Questions/Thoughts for Students

Algorithms sound fancy, but they are really just sets of rules that help sort data. Do you have any rules that help you sort and keep order? Do you put certain things in your room in certain places? Do you have routines that you do certain things first and then follow an order, such as when you get up in the morning?

Activity

With friends, take turns coming up with a category, like food, sports teams, or shopping. Each person writes down ten things that go in that category, and then arranges the list by two or three rules of their own. It can be from biggest to smallest, color, price, or what the person likes. You'll have to decide which rules go ahead of the others. For example, if you first sort by color but have two yellow fruits, the next rule says whichever is larger goes ahead.

Each person then takes a turn reading his or her list and the others try to guess what the rules of ranking are.

Follow-Up Questions/Discussions

Were some rules, like about the physical look of the objects, easier to figure out than rules about aspects you could not see, like which the person liked the most?

Was there disagreement, such as one person saying something was not as far away or as expensive or tasted as good as the person who made the list grouped them? What does that tell you about algorithms being objective?

The rules that you created, together, form an algorithm that then decides the order of the items. Try to think of another category and see if your algorithm can be used to sort out that category too.

When you do a search, the search results are sorted just like you did your category. The algorithm is much more complicated, but it might consider how popular sites are in putting them in order, or how many times the word you searched for appears on that site. Just like your algorithm, some rules may be clear, some may not be so clear.

LESSON 4L: YOUR GOOGLEGANGER IS SHOWING!

Focus of Exploration

Googleganger, misinformation on the internet

Intro Questions/Thoughts for Students

Have you ever met someone with the same first name as you? Did it cause confusion?

Have you ever met someone with the same last name as you, apart from your family? Is that rarer than meeting someone with the same first name as you? Did it cause confusion?

Have you ever met someone with the same first *and* last name as you?

Activity

Search your name. Try your formal first and last name and your nickname and last name. To narrow the search, put your full name in quotes so the search engine knows to look for the names together rather than a page that has both your first and last name scattered.

Look at the people who come up. If you get no hits, try your parents or other adults' names. What if someone thought you (or the other person) was the same as the person you found? Imagine what kind of confusion that would cause!

Follow-Up Questions/Discussions

There are a lot of stories about people who look alike switching places, like *The Prince and the Pauper*. Two people who look alike are called doppelgangers. Online, two people who have the same name are called **Googlegangers**.[1]

The lesson of Googlegangers is that we have to be careful. If we go too fast, we might grab the wrong person's information or make assumptions about a person because they have the same name as someone else. What can we do to not make that mistake?

---

1. There were three Jim Wassermans who wrote books at the same time just a few years ago. The Jim Wasserman who wrote this book used to get letters and asked questions that were meant for the other two.

If someone accidentally gets the wrong information, that is **misinformation**. If someone intentionally sends out bad information, that is **disinformation**. What can we do to make sure we don't fall for disinformation of someone pretending to be someone they are not online?

LESSON 4M: MEME'S THE WORD

Focus of Exploration

Power and limitations of memes

Intro Questions/Thoughts for Students

An old saying is that "a picture is worth a thousand words." What does that mean?

Jokes have a way of reducing big things to small but funny ideas. Why is that a good thing? Can it be bad, like leaving out too much? Has anyone made a joke about you and you thought it was unfair because it left out things?

Activity

Make a two-panel **meme**. The first should be titled "What I thought ___ would be like:" with a picture of how you envisioned something in your head. The second is "What it was actually like:" with a second picture of how you experienced it. Make the first one ideal and the other a wreck, or switch it the other way if it was surprisingly nice. You can use pictures from the internet or pictures of yourself.

Follow-Up Questions/Discussions

Did you make your meme funny or serious? Was it a funny complaint or a celebration of good things?

Why did you choose that topic? Is it the first thing that came to you, or is it one of the most important things in your life? Is it a popular topic you have seen elsewhere?

Do viewers of your meme comment more on the topic or the meme itself? What is the difference?

What factors about the topic were left out? Would someone who did not know you get an accurate picture of your life, or was that not the purpose of your meme? If memes are not meant to be specifically accurate but broader and more humorous, how can we make sure we don't take other people's memes as accurate and complete information?

People often use humor as a way to deal with problems or to complain. Why do we do that? Does it help to express our frustrations or help others understand our point of view? People sometimes add "kidding, not kidding" after a joke. Should jokes about a topic be used to get information about the subject? Why or why not?

LESSON 4N: MAYBE BABY

Focus of Exploration

Hedging

Intro Questions/Thoughts for Students

What are words that you say to mean that something is 100 percent, like *totally*, *completely*, or *guaranteed*? What are ways you say something is not 100 percent, like *probably*, *mostly*, or *maybe*? When people combine the two types of words, like saying something is *definitely possible*, what does that mean? Is it 100 percent?

Activity

Look for ads or statements in the news. A good source here are company statements about their products, like health food. Make expressions that say something is absolutely or 100 percent one color, and words and phrases that are less than 100 percent another color. Which do you see more of?

Follow-Up Questions/Discussions

When people use the less-than-100-percent words, they are giving themselves room to be wrong, called **hedging**. When is that OK to do? When is it good to do? When is it wrong to do?

What happens when you have a string of 100 percent words but with a hedge thrown in, like if something is "100 percent guaranteed, absolutely promised to *possibly* work"? In math, if you multiply a string of positive numbers, the product is a positive number. Throw in one negative number, like −1, and the whole product is negative no matter how many positive numbers were in the equation. Is a hedge among a string of 100 percent words like that? Why or why not?

When you talk with people they often—"often" is a hedge, BTW—will start by saying something is absolute or "always" that way. If you ask "Always?" they then back down and say, "Well, just about" or "Most of the time." Asking again makes them back off more sometimes (catch that hedge?). Why do people pull back like that? If they know what they say is not 100 percent, why do they start that way? Is it more emotion over reason? Does this show we should be careful of taking 100 percent remarks immediately as true, at least most of the time?

Companies mix a lot of 100 percent language with hedging in talking about their products. Sometimes, the 100 percent is said aloud and the hedge is put in small print at the bottom. Why do they do this? If they are trying to say that despite their 100 percent guarantee the product isn't 100 percent of what they say, at what point is it **disinformation**? If you see a company claim what you think is too much, write to them and tell them what you think!

LESSON 4O: JUST SAYIN'

Focus of Exploration

Innuendo

Intro Questions/Thoughts for Students

What does it mean to *imply* something (also known as **innuendo**)? How do people imply things? Why do people imply things rather than just say them?

You might hear people use the phrase "I'm just saying . . ." What does that mean? When they do say that, are they usually implying something else?

Activity

Look for statements in news and online, like in chat, where people are implying a second message or meaning to their words. For example, someone could say "Did you see John and Susie *together* last night?" They can also imply by leaving things out. If someone walks up to Jamal and Joe after a match and tells Jamal how well he played, but then just looks at Joe, could the speaker be implying something about Joe's play?

Look for different techniques that imply a message. One is **juxtaposition**, where two things are placed or mentioned together so you can compare, like Jamal and John above. Another is using a **rhetorical** answer that implies an answer, like "Are you really going to eat all that?"

Make a chart that quickly describes the situation, says what was stated and what was implied. You should also say whether you think it was wrong to imply that message and why.

Follow-Up Questions/Discussions

Mostly, people imply negative messages. Why do they do this? Sometimes positive messages are implied, like asking "Are you doing anything this weekend?" as a way to ask someone out. Why do we do that?

One reason for implying negative comments is to **hedge**, giving the speaker room to say "Oh no, I never meant that!" even if they did. What would you say to someone who implied something negative to you but then said they didn't mean it that way?

Sarcasm is a way to imply things by the tone of our voice, like saying "Oh yeah, I really *love* cleaning up everyone else's mess!" Is it harder to pick up implied meanings, even sarcasm, online in chats or in person? If it is harder online, what are the dangers then about implying things or using sarcasm there, such as in texting?

Chapter Five

Chat Talk

It was sometime around 2005 that the word *friend* went through a cultural change in meaning. Before, a *friend* was someone with whom we felt a connection. We knew them personally and they knew us, and both felt positive about it.

After 2005, a friend also became someone with whom we linked accounts on social media. Maybe they were someone we had seen in cyber passing or had mutual other friends online with. Maybe they were just someone who asked to link profiles. In any case, they were now a person's *friend*, and they could see your posts about your life and you could see theirs. *To friend* became an accepted verb, as did the gerund form of *friending* someone.

It was not only a linguistic shift but a cultural one as well. Few will remember proto-networking sites such as Six Degrees or Ryze, or making their first network friend, Tom, on Myspace. It was the rise of Facebook in the late 2000s that shifted the online world upon its axis, along with the concept of friend. Starting as a social connector for American college students, Facebook eventually opened its social media community to high schoolers and non-American university students in 2005. By 2006, any adult could have an account.

In those early days, the lure of social media was the ability to connect with so many people, and connect we all did. There were no degrees of friendship, just a friend or not. People could blast their presence to the world at large. The ability to tag people in photos created connections, especially as there was no limit to the number of photos one could post. By 2008, Facebook was the conqueror of the social media New World.

Young people especially loved Facebook back then. Looking for ways to prove their own social importance, combined with **aspirational motivation**[1] to imitate the college kids, teens and youth sought out as many friends as they could. They boasted when they got a hundred, then a thousand, friends. It didn't matter whether the young person actually knew or interacted with the person. It was the bragging rights of having that many connections. Social media was about how many people acknowledged, even minimally, that you existed.

Almost twenty years later, the feel of social media and how people, especially youth, see it and use it has changed. The thrill of having so many *friends* has long waned.[2] In fact, it became tiresome for many to have to scroll through so many posts by people they honestly didn't care that much about. Posts became repetitive, as one waded through an endless smorgasbord of pictures of the "one-of-a-kind meal" that every person posted.

People used other attention-getting devices like the **humblebrag**, as in "I really didn't think I could do it, but I am so honored to have been named the salesperson of the quarter." Many **overshared** personal details of their lives. Advertisers became adept at disguising ads as social media blasts. The videos and pitches were amusing at first—then they became intrusive.

There are other reasons Facebook lost youth appeal, including that it remained a text-based application with pictures supplementing. The next generation of users desired more visual communication, including having the ability to add filters and captions. This led to Instagram's and Snapchat's growth. Facebook has tried to update itself, even buying Instagram, but in the end, it seems Facebook cannot overcome the eternal uphill challenge of being seen as last generation's thing, with the next generation wanting their own brand.

See **Lesson 5A: Annoy-ments**.

There are now three levels of two-way communication that serve a communicator's different needs. Today, a person can communicate publicly so that anyone can see, semi-publicly in a chat space or group, or privately with one person or a few friends.[3]

Before we examine each level, we need to reemphasize that despite most every social media site having a stated minimum age of thirteen, kids under that age are chatting and communicating online. A 2018 study found that 93 percent of fourteen- to twenty-two-year-olds said they used social media.[4] It's hard to imagine that all those users, or even a majority of them, patiently waited until they met the thirteen-year-old threshold to start using social media. As discussed previously, we also know that many youth are going online with and without parental knowledge.

THE PUBLIC LEVEL OF COMMUNICATION

Facebook remains the largest social media platform. However, today its users skew to older, thirtysomething and above, age demographics.[5] The fact that Mom and Dad use Facebook as the family photo album, holiday letter, the "you'll never believe what my child did" notice board, etc., doesn't help its hipness. Facebook's utility as a communication forum is to stay connected with people who have moved away, maintaining the social fabric with the people who have touched our lives over the years. Kids don't need that yet.

Youth have little interest in chatting with the world at large today. Kids find more satisfaction in the intimacy of private communication like chatting in a group with friends.[6]

There is one thing about public communication youth need to be made aware of: They may be doing so without even knowing it. A young person can list all their social media accounts but might be hard-pressed to describe the **privacy settings** for each.

Even if the child is aware of what privacy settings are, they may think there is only one for each platform. In fact, most sites and platforms have subsettings that cover different aspects of what you do. Sometimes the settings default to public unless changed, which means anyone can see what the user says or does.[7] Someone out there may know more about a child's online activity than his or her parents do.[8]

See **Lesson 5B: It's a Family Thing**.

Why does it matter? A young person might well say they don't care who sees what they post, that they have nothing to hide. This is when the conversation can get tricky.

Everyone has things to hide, or at least to not share publicly. It doesn't mean what they are not revealing is wrong, just that it might be better to not share it. Let's say you are going shopping and you have a hundred dollars in your wallet. Is it a good idea to flash it around or yell out in public, "I got a hundred dollars in my wallet"? There are predators online. They are experienced and know how to look through postings for clues. The kid who complains about 6:00 a.m. swim practice at the local aquatics center every Saturday has given away a certain time and place they will be. Pictures of schoolmates often include a shirt or hoodie with the school's name on it.

See **Lesson 5C: Giveaways**.

Youth with public settings are not only leaving the door open for themselves, but for the rest of the family. Pictures will include family, but even more is that scammers and hackers look for public accounts to send entrapping messages. A predator might ask to follow or otherwise connect with a public account. Most kids, even while picky who their friends are IRL, accept follow and connection requests online knowing nothing about the person.

The scammer might follow that up with conversation or send a "cool link" to check out. In what is called **phishing** or **smishing**, clicking on the link can allow hackers to extract data or even place **malware** on the computer that can take control (including of the camera) or hold the computer for ransom. The whole family then pays the price.

See **Lesson 5D: Don't Go There!**

THE SEMIPUBLIC LEVEL OF COMMUNICATION

Kids, like adults, love to find commonality with others with the same interests. As we have said previously, tweens are discovering who they are and are hoping to form new "tribes" with those like them. Not only do they find friendship, but finding others with the same interests also reassures kids that they are not so different that they will be social outcasts.

It's one of the greatest gifts of the internet, discovering that you are not alone in your passion for something obscure like left-handed superheroes. Groups exist all over the internet for just about every interest or hobby. If you are a gamer and you want to talk about how cool or lame a game is, or how to beat a boss on level 10 of the dungeon, there will be a chat room on sites like Reddit. If you have a particular hobby or craft, or like pictures of cats, there is probably a group on Pinterest to share pictures and exchange ideas.

It's a world where kids can be kids with other kids or get guidance from acknowledged older veterans. Unfortunately, it's also a world where predators can pretend to be kids. As far back as 1993, the *New Yorker* published what is now a famous cartoon. It shows a dog, in front of a computer, a paw on the keyboard, saying to another dog, "On the Internet, no one knows you're a dog."[9] The cartoon illustrated the liberating freedom in being anonymous. People can try out different personalities. They can say and do things that social conventions IRL do not allow them to.

See **Lesson 5E: To Tell the Truth!**

The bad side of online anonymity is when people use it to **catfish**, to be someone they are not in order to take advantage of others. Imagine a park where twelve-year-olds hang out. Up walks a fifty-something-year-old guy. The guy can talk about the same K-pop bands or television shows the kids like. He seems nice if a bit strange. He then says he'd like to come and hang out at their house with them, since he claims to be the same age as them. Hopefully, the kids know enough to say no.

On the internet, however, youth may not know the guy is older. Don't get us wrong—the chat rooms and sites for common interests are in large part safe. However, there is a huge risk that wherever kids gather, so do predators, especially if they can connect without being seen.

Predators can, and unfortunately do, hide in plain sight—as well plain sites—in chat rooms. They talk with the kids, exchange jokes and ideas, all under the guise of being a kid or even a slightly older teen.[10] The experienced predator is patient, looking for signals the kid is unhappy or lonely. Over time, he can persuade the youth to go to private communication.

Tweens and other youth are intent on finding self-value but are inexperienced at social interaction. The predator, on the other hand, may be experienced and is looking for information to exploit. Kids will trust someone because the person is "nice" or listens to them and sympathizes with their problems like no one else does. The child might let their guard down slowly, then be talked into giving away more information or even becoming more intimate.

A survey of almost 4,000 children found that 43 percent of those aged between eight and thirteen were talking to people on social media and gaming platforms they had never met in real life. Of that percentage, the study found that more than half of the kids had revealed their phone number to a stranger, one-fifth had spoken with a stranger over the phone, and 11 percent went as far as to meet a stranger in their own home, the stranger's home, a park, or a mall.[11] The intimacy of sharing private information itself can be confused with romantic feelings.

If this all sounds like a bad teen drama, one needs to know it really happens. A lot. One in three young adults report having had an unwelcome sexual interaction online before they turned eighteen, and one in four children report that an adult has had a sexual interaction with them online.[12] Predators have coaxed children into sending explicit pictures or videos of themselves, which the predator then uses to blackmail the child.[13]

Preying on the young is not just about sex. Advocacy groups, including extremist ones, are now using online games and other chat areas to make connections and begin the process of swaying youth to embrace their views if not outright recruit kids as future members.[14] Parents may think their child is immune to hate messages or other extremism, but like any advertising, the goal is often not to win over a person in one message, but to be patient and instill the sway slowly, over time.

See **Lesson 5F: Twenty Questions for Parents**.

It's scary, but it doesn't mean that parents should lock the computer or phone away. It does mean that parents, teachers, and other adults need to be involved with children's communications. Parents need to know where their kids hang out, online and IRL.

Mostly, there needs to be an open relationship of communication. The children need to know that if they feel anything is amiss, they should trust their feelings and report it. They should be comfortable telling others *no* when asked to do things that they feel are not right. They also need to know that even if they dipped their toes in the water of "bad stuff," or even waded further in, it is never too late to reverse course and ask adults for a hand out of the sewage.[15]

See **Lesson 5G: Too Close!**

THE PRIVATE LEVEL OF COMMUNICATION

Most of the horror stories about kids chatting their way into trouble involve their interacting with adults. For the most part, however, kids are privately chatting and sharing pictures with their peers and friends. It's fun. It's helpful for school or to discuss problems. It builds friendships. It *is* the new friendship. In a 2018 survey, 61 percent of teens preferred texting their friends, video-chatting, or using social media over in-person communication.[16]

Used in moderation, texting and chatting with friends is beneficial.[17] Like anything, however, limits should be set to achieve a balanced life. Some kids experience bad **FOMO** if they don't keep checking their phone, even late into the night. The lure of the red dot and "ding" that signals one has a message is irresistible. Self-restraint is a learned skill.

Kids also need to be bilingual, able to communicate online and IRL. There are techniques and challenges to communicating in both "languages," and someone wishing to thrive in both worlds needs to know how to communicate well in both.

See **Lesson 5H: Being Bilingual**.

When communicating online, even privately, we all, but especially youth, need to be aware of some particular issues and take precautions. First and foremost, there really is no such thing as "private" online.[18] Once a text is out, it's almost impossible to undo it completely.[19] It can be shown, or screen-captured and shared. Context can be removed so that the surrounding chat that shows the text was a joke can be eliminated.[20]

Snapchat made its name because of its ephemeral nature of communication: The "snaps"—photos and videos—disappear after a short amount of time.[21] That feature, combined with the filters, captioning, and other fun add-ons, helped Snapchat to become one of the most popular apps for kids today. But do the snaps really disappear?[22] A receiver can still screenshot a snap. The sender is notified that a screenshot was taken, but there is little they can do.

Many kids today take a fatalistic attitude toward communication embarrassment. If it happens, it happens, and there is nothing they can do about it. To an extent they are correct that privacy isn't what it used to be for anyone. Still, we all can and should take precautions to protect our valuables, including data, reputations, and all else available for snatching online.

One of the challenges of online communication is the disconnect between how we see ourselves and what we text. In person, we literally stand behind our words as we say them, making us think more about what we are about to say and sometimes stopping ourselves short of regrettable statements. That one's name and reputation is associated with what we do has been a powerful check on people's behavior.[23]

We may want to say something in an emotional moment, like scream insults at another person. The knowledge that we will be judged poorly, however, often makes us stop, reflect, and find a better way to express ourselves. With the internet's anonymity, some have found no such self-check to keep from going too far, engaging in **trolling**, **flaming**, and otherwise **cyberbullying**.

Additionally, when we speak to someone face-to-face, we can't help but see their humanity. If we say something to upset them, we will see it in their face and know we went too far. Human brains seemed wired to prefer face-to-face contact.[24]

See **Lesson 5I: Victimless Crimes**.

Online, however, the person whom we are speaking to or saying bad things about is not in front of us. They then become an abstract idea that we can make fun of or ridicule, rather than a real person. They can become part of the vague group "them," rather than an individual with feelings and with their own point of view. It's easier to make a negative comment online than to an individual face-to-face. Many middle schoolers can recall walking into a room and watching a circle of schoolmates who were a moment ago feverishly gossiping about them suddenly stop and guiltily look at the person who just entered. Unleashing a small bit of negativity online can also set in motion, using the internet's multiplying force, a wave that becomes a tsunami of hate so terribly destructive that it can disrupt, even ruin, people's lives.[25]

See **Lesson 5J: Stop the Ripple, Stop the Wave**.

One last caution about two-way internet communication: It may seem to the average tween that saying something to a person's face and saying it to them in a chat or text amounts to the same thing. Legally, it is not. When one does something over the internet, one is using interstate communication. Threatening or bullying someone is wrong, and possibly even a state crime. Doing it online can also violate federal laws.[26] In any case, doing something on the internet is taking it public, which often ups the stakes in terms of crime and punishment.[27]

These are very serious consequences that need to be considered by kids who are just entering the adult world where "I'm sorry" may not be enough to resolve a matter. Youth aspire to have the freedom and power of teens and adults. They should understand, then, the adage repeated by so many but perhaps best succinctly put by Spider-Man, that with great power comes great responsibility. We also take for granted that while the ability to communicate comes naturally to most people, the ability to both communicate and listen, and to do both well, is an acquired skill.

See **Lesson 5K: Are You Joking?**

NOTES

1. Aspirational motivation is when someone makes choices in hopes of being more like someone they admire or living in what they consider a better way. It is an important driver of youth decision-making and is examined in detail in our companion book, *Behavioral Economics: A Guide for Youth in Making Choices.*

2. "Followers" are another matter.

3. We will address social media more broadly later. In this chapter, we are focusing on two way-communication.

4. Victoria Rideout and Susannah Fox, *Digital Health Practices, Social Media Use, and Mental Well-Being among Teens and Young Adults in the U.S.* (Hopelab and Well Being Trust, 2018), https://assets.hopelab.org/wp-content/uploads/2020/08/a-national-survey-by-hopelab-and-well-being-trust-2018.pdf.

5. S. Dixon, "U.S. Facebook Users by Age and Gender 2022," Statista, January 9, 2023, https://www.statista.com/statistics/187041/us-user-age-distribution-on-facebook.

6. The exception is in one-way shouting as a means of self-promotion to stardom, which we explore later.

7. Unfortunately, parents are often woefully negligent in using the available parental controls to help protect their children even when they know the child goes online unsupervised. National Poll on Children's Health, "Sharing Too Soon? Children and Social Media Apps," C. S. Mott Children's Hospital, October 18, 2021, https://mottpoll.org/reports/sharing-too-soon-children-and-social-media-apps.

8. As a test, we alternated setting our own Instagram account privacy settings between private and public. We had little unsolicited contact while our account was

private but were contacted numerous times, sometimes multiple times in one day, by scammers and other unsavory people when our account was public.

9. Wikipedia, "On the Internet, Nobody Knows You're a Dog," last modified January 10, 2020, https://en.wikipedia.org/wiki/On_the_Internet,_nobody_knows _you%27re_a_dog.

10. Being a teen often makes them more enticing to a tween.

11. Madison Forster, "How Many Kids Give Away Information to Strangers?" Savvy Cyber Kids, July 21, 2022, https://savvycyberkids.org/2022/07/21/how-many -kids-give-away-information-to-strangers.

12. ParentsTogether Action, "Parent Advisory: 2021 Sets Records for Child Sexual Abuse Online; 3x Increase in Sexual Images of 7–10 Year Olds," January 18, 2022, https://parentstogetheraction.org/2022/01/18/parent-advisory-2021-sets-records-for -child-sexual-abuse-online.

13. One in five nine- to twelve-year-olds report being asked for "nudes" or other sexual acts online. A sign of how common it is to exchange intimate pictures is the common online acronym GNOC for "get naked on camera (or cam)."

14. Anya Kamenetz, "Right-Wing Hate Groups Are Recruiting Video Gamers," NPR, November 5, 2018, https://www.npr.org/2018/11/05/660642531/right-wing -hate-groups-are-recruiting-video-gamers.

15. Kids don't like to be told "You're just a kid," except when they have been led astray by older people. Then, "You're just a kid" can become a reassuring message that it is not their fault.

16. Mariel Loveland, "Teens Would Rather Text and Chat Online with Their Friends Than Hang Out in Real Life, Study Says," Insider, September 12, 2018, https://www.insider.com/study-teens-would-rather-text-with-friends-than-hang-out -in-real-life-2018-9.

17. And again, because we can't say it enough, all under the watchful eye of parents. Many parents have kids place their phones in a common charging area at night so they cannot text in their room. Parents also work in cooperation with each other, letting others know what they see.

18. One could say the two biggest lies of the online world are that anything is private or that anything is deleted.

19. Though this ability is starting to be introduced, such as with the latest Apple phones if both the text sender and receiver have iOS 16 or later.

20. This is beside the fact that most social apps and text programs back up their data, including messaging, on servers. Also, depending how your text is routed, such as through a business or school network, those servers can retain a copy.

21. It is why their mascot is a ghost, to symbolize the disappearance.

22. Unopened snaps are kept stored on Snapchat's servers for up to thirty days.

23. In the negative, communities have used public identification as a tool of repression to "out" people for saying or going against the norms of the community.

24. Matt Villano, "Why Hanging Out Face-to-Face Still Matters," CNN, June 8, 2021, https://www.cnn.com/2021/06/07/health/face-to-face-brain-wellness-scn/ index.html.

25. It's important to note that the reasons people cyberbully are as varied as the people themselves. Parents should monitor what their children do, but if they see any indication they are involved in bullying, we highly recommend that they seek out a counselor on the child's behalf. If parents suspect their child is being bullied, they should similarly consult a counselor at their child's school or find an independent one as soon as possible.

26. There is not a specific federal anti-bullying law, but some bullying can implicate discriminatory harassment laws covered under federal civil rights laws.

27. In many states, laws against child pornography do not exempt the person pictured from culpability. Thus, a minor who sends or posts a nude selfie can be considered in violation of child pornography laws (subject to age-limit culpability as a juvenile).

Chapter 5 Accompanying Lessons

LESSON 5A: ANNOY-MENTS

Focus of Exploration

Oversharing, self-serving statements online

Intro Questions/Thoughts for Students

Has someone ever told you something and you wondered why they were telling it to you?

Has anyone ever told you things about their life that made you uncomfortable because you didn't want to know, or the topic made you uncomfortable?

Activity

Look through chat discussions on social media or perhaps a general posting site and find posts that you do not like. Perhaps they are annoying announcements, or *annoy-ments*. Look for patterns in what bothers you. Are they people bragging too much? Perhaps they are offensive or mean, or they **overshare** by telling too much information that makes you feel uncomfortable?

The key here is not just identifying what posts annoy or bother you. It is for you to reflect on *why* they bother you.

Follow-Up Questions/Discussion

The first step is to think about how much of the bad feeling comes from the post and how much from how you are taking it. For example, you could read something as annoying bragging, but it might be that you are a bit jealous of their success. It also depends on how close you are with the person saying it. If a friend describes how sick they were, with details, we are more tolerant than if a stranger tells us about it.

Do you hear more bragging, oversharing, and other bothersome statements online or in person? If online, what about being online might cause it? Is it that we cannot see the other person to know we have crossed the line? Is it that we are so into our own space we forget to consider how the audience might take our message? Maybe it's the seemingly limitless space to get our thoughts out?

Many bothersome posts are created when the poster was overcome with a strong feeling or emotion and that makes them brag, overshare, be mean, or say other things that a moment's cool pause might have prevented. What does this teach you about posting or texting when you are emotional or not thinking?

How can you politely tell someone that you don't care for a post or text, or that it bothers you? When is it important that you should say something? When is it better to let it go? Does it depend on whether it hurts someone else, or even the poster themself?

We mostly cannot change what other people post or text, but by seeing bothersome posts we can learn how we can communicate better. For example, if someone says they regretted the next day what they quickly posted the night before, what lesson can you take from that? If you wonder why the person didn't think about how readers might take his or her post, or the effect the post would have on others' feelings, does that tell you to think about it in your own communication? If you read the post of someone being mean or unkind and it makes you think less of the poster, what do you learn from that?

Wisdom comes from looking back at past mistakes. A good source of wisdom in online communication are kids slightly older than you who have lived to see the good and bad consequences of what they did online. Ask teens what advice they would give someone your age about being online. What advice would they have about chatting, gaming, or watching movies? Looking back, what would they have done differently? What should you look forward to doing? Of course, you can put in your own questions that you have or maybe something you are particularly concerned about, such as bullying or if they ever lost a friend because of something said online.

LESSON 5B: IT'S A FAMILY THING

Focus of Exploration

Privacy settings

Intro Questions/Thoughts for Students

What are **privacy settings**? What do they do? Why do they matter? Do you know how to find or change privacy settings?

Activity

Everyone in the family should list their favorite sites or apps that they use. Put them all on one list. Then, for each, look at the privacy settings as a group to see who is seeing or could potentially be seeing all that is being done on that app or site. Which activities are the most private? Which are the most public? As a family decision, should any be changed?

Follow-Up Questions/Discussions

Why is it important to do a privacy check as a whole family? Think of one person leaving a door into the house unlocked. Does that affect everyone's security?

In judging how public a post or picture is, what is the difference between how many people could potentially see it and how many have actually viewed it? Why is that important?

Has anyone made a comment or posted a picture about someone else in the family? Should the family member referred to or shown be able to say take it down? Should your family have a general agreement about referring to or showing other members?

If anyone wants to change the privacy settings for their account on a site, have a family discussion about the pluses and minuses, costs, and benefits of changing the settings, both for the family member and for the family as a whole.

LESSON 5C: GIVEAWAYS

Focus of Exploration
Privacy online

Intro Questions/Thoughts for Students

What can you tell about a person just by looking at them? Sherlock Holmes could tell a lot. For example, in one story he saw a person had an expensive jacket that had a patch, so he concluded that the man was once well-to-do but had fallen on hard times.

What can you tell about a person by seeing things in their posts? Can you tell where they live or where they work or go to school?

Activity

Pretend you are a detective. You are assigned to find out all you can about someone. Choose a friend of yours to be the "unknown person." Look at their posts and all online activity. Look at things like their saying in chats where they will be or who they will be with, often as a casual comment. If you did not know them, could you by their posts figure out:

- Where they live, either by city or even down to the area of town or address?
- Where they go to school?
- What activities they like?
- Details about their family or friends?
- When they are home and where they are at certain times?

Photos also show more than we intend. Your friend could be wearing a school uniform, or another person in the photo could have on a school shirt (perhaps the same school or club the subject person belongs to). Look for clues and signs in the background of the pics.

Follow-Up Questions/Discussions

You are just finding out information, but can someone use such information to hurt your friend if they wanted to? Now do the same for your own texts and posts.

We want to be able to share the things going on in our lives, but we also need a balance. Does it matter if the pics and text you looked at are marked as public or private? Did you check that? Does your friend know whether what he or she posts is public or private? Do you know about yours?

The risk is not just online. Parents brag about their child being an honor student at a particular school or participating in an activity on the back of their cars. When might it be too much? How can we strike a balance?

We also can reveal what we think, our values, or what kind of person we are. Many celebrities have been undone by showing that they are not a nice person from their posts. For your subject that you looked at, do they seem like a positive or negative person by their posts? Do they accurately communicate their values?

LESSON 5D: DON'T GO THERE!

Focus of Exploration

Phishing and smishing

Intro Questions/Thoughts for Students

Have you ever had someone you don't know walk up to you and speak? How did that feel? Weird? What did you do? Did you keep your guard up? How long?

Have you ever been in a situation where a social interaction didn't feel right? Where maybe you thought there was something being hidden, or someone wasn't being honest? What were the clues that made you feel that way?

Activity

As a family activity, discuss getting emails and texts from strangers, or unexpected communication from friends. How often do the adults get them? What do they do? Do the kids ever get them? Most importantly, do they ever get email (**phishing**) or text (**smishing**) with links in them? What harm can come from clicking on them?

The family should discuss how each knows or suspects something is off. For example, an email can come from what seems like a major corporation, but the sending address is not from that company. Also, customer support numbers are given but you know that the company—because you first checked—doesn't have telephone support. Maybe you get a text that doesn't use your name but asks "Is this YOU?!" with a link. Together, the family should develop a list of "best practices" or red flags to look for that will be written and followed when anyone gets a phish or smish and then alert the others.

Follow-Up Questions/Discussions

As we said previously, these exercises are important for the entire family to do because the family computer or device, if unguarded, is like an unlocked door that bad guys can enter to get to everyone.

An extra minute of double-checking can save a whole lot of pain. Even when you are in a hurry, you take a minute to look both ways before crossing a street. We take a minute to buckle seat belts and to look through peepholes before opening front doors. Online, we can text a friend "Did you just send me something?" before opening a link. Some people have a hard "I don't click on sent links" rule. What other best practices can you think of for responding to messages?

Car safety people came up with "click it or ticket" to raise awareness of using seat belts. Can you come up with a campaign for message safety for your school to use?

Part of the problem of scammers sending bad links is that if they hack a friend's computer, they can send a text pretending to be your friend sending a link. Has that ever happened to you or a member of your family? How can you double-check that it is your friend sending you the link? Besides contacting your friend separately, can you agree to a code or letter signal in a message to know it is from them? A cartoon many years ago showed how even dogs can disguise who they are online![1] Maybe you can make a cartoon or write a short story that is funny but also has a warning about impersonating.

---

1. Wikipedia, "On the Internet, Nobody Knows You're a Dog," last modified January 10, 2020), https://en.wikipedia.org/wiki/On_the_Internet,_nobody_knows_you%27re_a_dog.

LESSON 5E: TO TELL THE TRUTH!

Focus of Exploration

Looking for tells in judging who is telling the truth

Intro Questions/Thoughts for Students

Are you good at spotting when someone is making things up or not telling the truth?

"Tells" are little clues or giveaways in a person's behavior that signal they are bluffing or not telling the truth. For example, a person may look nervous and their eyes shift, or they may rub their eyebrow as they make something up. What are the tells of the people you know?

Activity

This is based on an old TV game show, *To Tell the Truth*. Have three people line up for questioning. Before questioning, the three should agree to a fact that is true for one of them, like having met a famous movie star or their team went to the state championship. Make sure no one on the questioning panel knows which person it is true for.

The three then go in front of a panel of at least three people. The panel is told the general premise, such as that one of these people met a famous movie star and talked with them. The panel then asks questions, one each in rotation. The person who must answer rotates, so the first question goes to testifier #1, the second question to #2, then #3, and then back to #1. Each questioner gets at least three questions and can ask whatever they want, even repeating a question but to another person.

Importantly, the person for whom the statement is true must answer every question truthfully. The other two can say whatever they want to and obviously make up a story and try to be convincing.

The panel then votes on who they think the story is true for. Once revealed, discuss why the panel went the way they did and discuss any tells they picked up.

Follow-Up Questions/Discussions

Asking "Are you telling the truth?" is not helpful. Why not? What are better questions?

The longer someone speaks, the easier it is to pick up tells. Which is better, then, yes/no questions or open-ended ones that get the responder to say things at length?

It's also hard, when making up things, to remember what you said before and not contradict yourself. Why, then, is it a good strategy to follow up on someone else's question and ask someone to talk further about it or to add on to it?

Do you notice any tells that many people have in common that they are not telling the truth? Speaking too fast or slowly? Overexplaining or diverting the question to something else?

All of this was face-to-face. Is it easier or harder to tell if someone is telling the truth online? Why? In a face-to-face conversation, we normally respond right away and can't stop to fact-check or ask someone else to help verify a story. Is that an advantage of the internet? How can it be used?

LESSON 5F: TWENTY QUESTIONS FOR PARENTS

Focus of Exploration

Parental awareness of children's social connections

Intro Questions/Thoughts for Students

How much do your parents know about what you do online? Do they know who you mainly communicate with? What apps or sites you use?

How much do you think your parents should be generally aware of what you do online? Maybe not what you specifically text, but generally whom you text with?

Activity

Kids should answer all of the following:

- My favorite thing to do online is:
- The site or app I use most online is:
- The site or app I use second most online is:
- For most research questions, I use this site:
- My favorite chatting site/app/group is:
- My favorite online source for music is:
- My favorite band/performer is:
- I spend about ___ hours online during weekdays.
- I spend about ___ hours online each day on weekends.
- The two people I talk with most online are:
- My favorite person to watch online is:
- My favorite person most often talks about the topic of:
- I have been bullied, harassed, or embarrassed online (Y/N).
- I have been bullied, harassed, or embarrassed online by someone I know IRL (Y/N).
- I have been threatened online (Y/N).
- I have chatted with people I do not know personally online (Y/N).
- I have seen things online that have made me worried about a friend's health or safety (Y/N).
- If I wanted to talk about concerns or worries I have about things I have seen or happened to me online, I would talk with:
- If I could ask my parents to do one thing to make my online activity better, I would ask them to:

Kids should then have parents answer these questions, guessing what their kids would say. Grade your parents and let them know their score out of 20.

Follow-Up Questions/Discussions

Hiding or at least not telling parents everything that you do or what goes on is very normal for kids. You want and are entitled to a degree of privacy. However, if you do withhold something from your parents, it's important to ask why you don't want to tell them. For example, if you like doing something but don't think your parents will approve, you might consider what your parents may know that you don't, like some hidden harm. You also might be surprised that your parents support your liking it! You should also think of someone you can talk with, like a school counselor, should you need advice or guidance.

Big topics like what you should and should not do online can't usually be resolved in one discussion. Sometimes it's better to talk a little bit and then stop and have everyone reflect and come back to it. Also, situations change. Maybe you can set up a talk every six months or so to discuss the "State of the Internet" to review how things are going and what needs updating.

It's a good rule of thumb IRL to let parents know where you are going when you go places. Does the same apply when you go to places online? Why or why not?

LESSON 5G: TOO CLOSE!

Focus of Exploration

Comfort with personal subjects

Intro Questions/Thoughts for Students

Are there some personal subjects you feel more comfortable talking about than others?

Do people sometimes bring up personal subjects you don't want to talk about? When has that happened? What did you do?

Activity

This is an imagination experiment that requires a partner.

On a large piece of paper, draw a circle as big as you can. Put a dot in the middle and six lines that go from the circle inward to meet at the dot.

You are to imagine yourself standing at the center of the circle. For each line, there is a person you are to imagine who wants to ask you questions about a topic. Your partner will announce the topic and say "Go," starting a timer. You then imagine that person asking you questions, taking a step closer and closer to you as their questions get more and more personal about that topic.

Don't say the questions you imagine or your answers out loud but imagine having to. When you feel uncomfortable about being in that situation and discussing that topic, say "Stop!" Your partner should record the time (without letting you see). Clear your head and then repeat for the rest of the topics. Set a maximum for any one topic at two minutes.

When finished, you will have a list of the six topics and the time for each. Now plot the distance you allowed the person to mentally approach by the time. If you let it go two minutes, they are right next to you. If you let them question you for one minute, they came halfway.

The topics that the person wants to ever more intensely talk with you about are:

- Your family, each member and how you feel about them, what you do.
- Who you like and dislike, including who you are maybe attracted to.
- Your favorite passion or hobby, maybe even one no one knows about.
- What you know about your friends and classmates, including any secrets or gossip you might have heard about them.

- What your personal dreams and hopes are for what you want to be as an adult.
- What you do on the weekends, including where you will be, who you will be with, and what you will do there.

Follow-Up Questions/Discussions

Psychologists, therapists, and philosophers use exercises like these, called *thought experiments*, to try to get people to focus and reflect on things that are hard to think about. Did you find it hard to imagine yourself in these situations? Why or why not?

Did you imagine the same kind of person asking you the different questions? Did you imagine a person you knew or a stranger? Would your answers be different if you imagined a different person questioning?

We had you imagine a person in front of you. How would it change if the questions came online, still getting more personal with each question but texted to you? Do you think you would be more open to reveal things? Why or why not? Is that a good idea?

Can some of the things that you are more comfortable with be dangerous to reveal in some circumstances? For example, if you said exactly what you do and where you will be on the weekend to a stranger, could someone with bad intent use that against you?

Most importantly, when someone, either in person or online, starts to ask you questions to the point that you feel uncomfortable, how can you tell them to stop or remove yourself from the situation? Perhaps come up with a strategy and practice it.

What if you said you didn't want to discuss something, and the person then said they wouldn't be your friend anymore unless you answered? What if they said your not answering makes them feel like you don't trust them? How would you respond?

LESSON 5H: BEING BILINGUAL

Focus of Exploration

Language online

Intro Questions/Thoughts for Students

Do you speak or are you learning a second language? Spanish? French? Chinese? Do you look for similar words in both languages that help you, like that "no" sounds similar in many Western languages and means the same thing? What about "cat"?

When you learn a language, do you compare it to your native language so you can understand similar ideas? Are there any ideas in one language that are hard to translate because they're not quite the same idea in your native tongue?

Activity

Create a RW/O (real world/online) dictionary to help others translate and understand the languages of the two worlds. List important words or phrases that you use online and their meaning. Then list how the same ideas are conveyed in the real world.

For online, be sure to include shorthand abbreviations like LOL or BRB. Also include emojis. For the real world, remember we also use body language, including our hands and facial expressions, to convey meaning.

Follow-Up Questions/Discussions

Just like learning a second spoken language, it's really cool to be able to communicate with someone else in another language. Do you enjoy communication in *onlinese*? Is it a kind of "our thing" way of speaking that bonds you and your friends? Do other languages or individual words, like slang, do that for you? Have you ever started to use a word to be a part of a group?

Words have both *denotations*, which are the strict meaning of words, and *connotations*, which are deeper implied meanings. For example, LOL's denotation is "laugh out loud," meaning it's funny. The connotation is that the two people communicating share the same sense of humor and they are bonding over a shared funny thing. "Sketchy" is not just a way to say something is amiss or off. The connotation is that the person who says this is questioning the appropriateness or legitimacy of the situation. What other words online have extra connotations?

In spoken languages, words from other languages get adopted and absorbed over time. The English word for burrito is . . . burrito (which goes back to Spanish for "little donkey"). What internet words and phrases have you heard used in spoken language IRL? If you watch two people who both speak multiple languages talk, they often switch between the languages, even within one sentence. Do you do that with friends who know *onlinese*?

For extra fun, write out phrases in your spoken language and have people translate them on the spot into *onlinese* (perhaps with a projected screen so people can see what is written). You could also do a skit involving visitors to the online world and needing a translator.

LESSON 5I: VICTIMLESS CRIMES

Focus of Exploration

Self-regulation of behavior

Intro Questions/Thoughts for Students

We normally think of crimes as bad because they hurt someone else right away. If you steal, you have taken something from someone else. There are other things that are considered crimes or wrong, however, because they can hurt the person who is doing it, like doing drugs. There can also be a victim or someone who is indirectly hurt down the line, like with pollution. They are sometimes called "victimless crimes" although as we said either the person doing it or someone else eventually becomes a victim. What other kinds of actions would you classify as victimless crimes for either hurting the person doing it or someone else eventually?

Activity

Make a list of things people tell you are bad to do online or specifically on social media. For each, decide who is the victim or hurt by the action. Are they victimless crimes in that they hurt the person doing them or will they harm someone else indirectly? Are there any where you don't see the harm?

Follow-Up Questions/Discussions

One of the reasons for age limits is that a person too young to understand what they are doing may hurt themself or cause damage. Someone under sixteen might be physically able to drive in an empty parking lot, but they might not be able to handle a car when there are other vehicles, hitting and hurting someone else. What age limits can you think of that fit that? Ask adults what possible dangers are there that a young person might not see.

Youth also don't think about how doing something can hurt their reputation or future by a bad act. Have you seen where someone didn't think about the consequences of what they did? Ask your parents if they know of people who unintentionally caused harm to their own reputation by a bad act. Are such acts victimless crimes?

Sometimes people risk doing hurtful things to others or even themselves because "everyone does it." Is that an OK excuse? If you join in doing something harmful, can you be sending the message that it's OK for others to do it?

If you saw a friend doing things online that you thought could be harmful to them or hurt someone indirectly, what would you do? Can you talk to the person? Is there someone you could go to for advice on how to handle it? When is it better to get involved?

LESSON 5J: STOP THE RIPPLE, STOP THE WAVE

Focus of Exploration

Stopping online activity from getting out of hand

Intro Questions/Thoughts for Students

Have you ever seen a small incident blow up and get out of control, like a small disagreement turning into a big fight? When those kinds of things blow up, is there one big explosion or does it grow and build until it is out of hand?

When should you wait to see if something that could get out of hand actually does? When should you try to do something before it gets out of hand?

Activity

Think of things you don't like to see people doing online, including yourself. Think about people being mean, arguing, bullying, taking a prank too far, gossiping, embarrassing someone or making them feel uncomfortable by getting too personal, and any other behaviors that make you uncomfortable.

For each of these waves of negativity, think about how they start. While they are still ripples that are manageable, what can be done to stop them before they turn into big waves? Perhaps you can say "That's too much" or "Hey, let's stop." Maybe even say "I'm not comfortable with this, I'm leaving the chat"? Write out your methods and statements that might work with each kind of ripple, and keep it nearby to refer to when needed.

Follow-Up Questions/Discussions

Sometimes people don't want to admit publicly they are bothered by something. They don't want to be the "fun killer." To help, friends sometimes work out a code word so they can say to one another "I am not comfortable with what is going on. Help me!" Maybe you and your friends can come up with one?

Things often seem to get out of hand more quickly online than in real life. Perhaps it is that so many people can be involved in a chat that it is magnified. Since everyone is separated, there is no group feeling that the situation is getting out of hand or that real feelings are being hurt. What can you do to make it easier to stop ripples growing into waves online?

Is doing nothing when you see bad things starting as bad as helping? When is doing nothing to stop a ripple growing like saying it's OK to do? When is it OK, even perhaps better, to not step in?

One suggestion for knowing whether something is OK to do is from philosopher Immanuel Kant. If you want to know if a behavior is OK, you have to imagine that everyone is allowed to do it. Does that help you decide when something is going too far? There's also the Golden Rule, to ask when seeing how others are treated if you would be OK if you were treated that way or would you want watchers like yourself to step in to help.

Instead of focusing only on stopping bad ripples, how about starting some good ones that grow into positive waves? Write a list of ten places or people you like. For the places, find their website and leave a positive review. Let them know you like them, and help their business by letting others know. You can also leave positive reviews on guides such as Google Maps. If it's a book or something you bought, leave a positive review where it is sold online. For the people you listed, text them either privately or by leaving a comment. Try to make it personal by specifically identifying aspects of them you think are cool or why you like them.

LESSON 5K: ARE YOU JOKING?

Focus of Exploration

Determining intent online

Intro Questions/Thoughts for Students

When talking with someone face-to-face, how can you tell when the other person is joking, serious, or being sarcastic? What are the clues that you use?

Is it harder to tell if someone is joking or being sarcastic online? Why or why not?

Activity

Write out phrases on slips of paper like "I like your clothes," "Let's get together soon," "I care," or even "Thanks a lot!" On other slips of paper, write out "serious," "sarcastic," "joking," "angry," and "happily enthusiastic." One person draws a statement slip and an emotion slip. They have to then say that, and everyone has to guess which emotion they were imitating.

Now repeat but the person has to text the statement and convey the emotion.

Follow-Up Questions/Discussions

Is it easier to figure out how a statement was meant in real life or online? Why?

How can you tell how a statement was intended online? What emotions are hardest to figure out online? We sometimes use emojis and other symbols, but sometimes we leave them out. Is there a way then to know how a statement was intended?

A lot of meaning comes not just from the sentence itself but from the context or situation in which it is used. That includes what you know of the speaker. Is it harder to figure out context IRL or online? Why?

Chapter Six

How Influencers Hold Sway

Beginning with a patent filed in 1911 for the first modern loudspeaker,[1] people saw the potential of electronic public address (PA) systems for reaching a large audience at one time. Charles Comiskey installed one of the first PA systems for his Chicago White Sox baseball team's new stadium in 1913.

In the 1920s and 1930s, use of electronic voice broadcasting took off. Radio brought people's voices from around the world into living rooms, followed by "talkie" movies in theaters. As people for the first time could hear their sports and entertainment heroes, they began to feel more connected with them. Celebrity marketing discovered a powerful combination of broadcasting to everyone while allowing, even inviting, individuals to imagine what the star must be like out of the spotlight.

In 1923, Calvin Coolidge became the first US president to speak on radio. It's hard to imagine that this was the first time a majority of Americans could know what their leader's voice sounded like.[2]

By the 1930s, most politicians were aware that the booming sound of a PA system not only broadcast and amplified a person's words, but could also create an audio image.

See **Lesson 6A: Look of a Leader**.

President Franklin Roosevelt was a master at crafting a public image as he guided the country through the Great Depression and World War II.[3] He always made sure to be pictured smiling and optimistic. Even more, he used the power of radio to give reassuring addresses to the public with his fireside chats. In a technique that presaged internet videos, Franklin's radio addresses allowed people to hear their national leader but in the intimacy of their own home. He was both the grand national leader and the personal consoler.[4]

See **Lesson 6B: Theaters of the Mind**.

FDR's combination of broad leadership and intimate connection has been a successful formula ever since. However impactful it was to hear national personalities on the radio, it was increased by seeing such people on television.

Politicians like John Kennedy tapped into it, showing pictures of himself being a leader but also playing with his children. Similar to *photogenic*, a new term, *telegenic*, was coined for people like Kennedy who looked good on TV. Meanwhile, his wife, First Lady Jacqueline Kennedy, was also telegenic and admired. Women wanted to imitate her style, her dress, and her manner. People both looked up to and felt a connection with the Kennedys, demonstrated by their being affectionately referred to as "Jack and Jackie."

Entertainment celebrities also tapped into the power of **fake intimacy**. Magazines gave peeks into celebrities' lives "off camera," even if those peeks were scripted and designed. An entire subgenre of such magazines, the tween or "teeny bop" magazine, told youth about pop stars' and other celebrities' secret fears or crushes.

See **Lesson 6C: Inside Scoop**.

Television shows became as much about the personality hosting it as the show itself. As many people referred to the top late-night talk show as "Johnny Carson" or "Carson" as they did its official name, *The Tonight Show*. News and commentary programs across the political spectrum today are still driven by people's attachment to the host as much as the content.

See **Lesson 6D: Just Like You**.

Today, parents are worried about kids being negatively swayed by internet **influencers**. In many ways, it's the same as it ever was. Young fans look up to the influencers, wanting to know all about them, including what they are like off-screen. The seemingly shared views, interests, and humor of **content creators** sway young viewers to wonder if an online media personality understands them better than their parents or other people the kid knows IRL.

WHO ARE INFLUENCERS TODAY?

To be as succinct as possible, an influencer is someone whose popularity affects the outlook and choices of large cross sections of society. The choices can be personal, such as fashion, or be about things on a broader scale, such as politics. The influencer has some sort of media platform, nowadays often on the internet, from which they **nudge** and **sway** their audience by recommending things, giving their opinion on matters, or modeling.

Influencing is not just a by-product of being popular. It is now an established online profession and career path, especially as seen by young people. Musicians and others with talent can be popular and therefore influential in other ways for their fans. Taylor Swift became an influencer this way. Some influencers start their path by being personable and then use that to jump to celebrity and influencer status.

Once one is seen as an influencer, they can pick up sponsors who will pay them to use their influence for the sponsor's benefit. There is no set number or measure by which a popular person on the internet, social media, or IRL becomes an official influencer. It is a generally designated title, though rough delineations, such as micro and nano influencer, are beginning to develop.

Influencers, then, are spokespeople, pushing products, points of view, or even themselves. In old marketing days, spokespeople were basically one of two types. One was the celebrity, who used their public clout to endorse a product, candidate, or other choice. The other kind was a "plain folks" spokesperson who spoke on an even level to the audience, like a neighbor recommending something.[5]

On today's internet, influencers can be both kinds of spokespeople at the same time. The influencer is a known name with a large platform, yet by virtue of the fake intimacy of internet videos coming into people's homes, he or she comes off as a relatable neighbor personally recommending something.

In many ways, today's influencer was born because celebrity became so universal in the early days of the World Wide Web, the next generation longed for something more personal and intimate, or at least appearing that way. People sought out like-minded persons and began to create subcommunities and niches virtually. They also looked for spokespeople who could speak to and for that particular group. Even if such a celebrity amassed thousands of followers, they were still, to the subgroup, "theirs" and not part of the greater world of disassociated hawkers yelling for them to consume whatever they universally pushed to everyone.

Such influencers have **personal celebrity**. They are recognized and authoritative celebrities, but only within an in-crowd. The followers then consider themselves special and cool because they know of the influencer.[6] Influencers create content appealing to their followers' particular interests and tastes. They also recount personal, relatable stories, such as when mega-influencer PewDiePie[7] described how he initially created a YouTube account but had to create a whole new one, his current one, because he forgot the password of his old one.

Marketing done by an in-your-face plug has proven less effective today than if done by under-the-radar, subtle recommendation. It can be an influencer off-handedly recounting how great the product is for them, or just the product's ever-presence on-screen. Interestingly, surveys of tweens show that one of the things they dislike most about watching videos is ad interruption. They don't seem to realize the subtle ads built in.

See **Lesson 6E: Under the Influencer**.

WHAT MAKES AN INFLUENCER SUCCESSFUL?

There are so many types of influencers plying their personalities in so many ways up and down the internet, it would be difficult to universalize what makes them successful. However, one word that keeps rising in interviews with followers is **authenticity**. Being authentic, so that people feel like they are getting the real story, coming from a real person, is a foundation of building trust that leads to acceptance of the messenger and the message.

Young people have collectively said they long for honesty or at least what can pass for it.[8] In a time-crunched world, even adults don't have the time or energy to wade through generic, disingenuous pitches. For kids who learn that not all older people can and should be trusted, they are looking for anchors they can rely on. So great is the pushback against fake, **curated** posts that an app[9] was created in which people take real photos of what they are doing and as they really look at random times of the day.

Of course, marketers, knowing this, have gotten good at pretending to be authentic. Because the influencer seems so casual and real, viewers forget that the influencer is a salesperson. Their clothes are carefully chosen, as is every brand one sees in the video. Even what seems like an unscripted (**impromptu**) mention is probably scripted. Influencers do that because they have sponsors who pay them to mention or show off a brand, not necessarily because the influencer really likes it. Of course, the influencer doesn't know his or her audience personally, so any obligation to be honest as with a real friend is not there.[10]

See **Lesson 6F: Paid to be Authentic**.

Becoming a successful influencer requires an ability to connect with the audience. There are people we listen to because we believe they know what they are talking about, but we wouldn't quite say we "follow" or are "fans" because we don't feel a connection other than respecting their knowledge or authority.

For influencers, a personable connection is key to having people come back. Somehow, the influencer has to create a person-to-person affinity across the internet. There are techniques to doing it, including an open body position and eye contact, as well as speaking in a relaxed, conversational tone with vocabulary similar to that used by the audience.

See **Lesson 6G: Make Your Own Authentic, Non-Made, Video**.

Experienced conversationalists know that dialogue has to be a two-way flow. People want to be heard. This is difficult when one is broadcasting on the internet, but good influencers know how to do it. They read off comments or name-drop a fan who sent a message. They indicate they know the fans are out there, appreciate their attention, and otherwise acknowledge the audience. The gratitude is at least partially sincere—they couldn't be influencers without people to influence—but these reach-outs and shout-outs also work to bring the audience in, both those who are mentioned and those who hope for a mention in the future.

See **Lesson 6H: How Is the Internet Connection?**

If the influencer is successful at making connections, they then wield the marketing power of **brand loyalty**. The decision to follow the influencer becomes a fan's nonthinking, go-to choice. This can be a good thing, as it saves choosers time from having to reweigh choices every single time, and can even give them a sense of identity. It can also be a trap of habit.

Influencers don't have to work as hard as competitors to keep fans from watching something else as they become the choice of habit. Normally, consumers look at the quality of a product and then decide if the seller is good. Once brand loyalty attaches, consumers start with liking the seller and then assume everything he or she has is good.

Brand loyalty also compels fans to be more willing to forgive an influencer's mistakes or even serious errors in judgment. PewDiePie is known for sponsoring and staging pranks which are mostly harmless. One prank in 2017 involved displaying an anti-Semitic sign. Also in 2017, he used a racial slur while live-streaming his gameplay.

In both cases, though he was severely criticized and lost some sponsorship, PieDiePie's loss of followers was minimal and forgiving. In fact, many fans later reacted positively because he posted apologies and fans, especially male ones, felt a kinship. They empathized with thinking a borderline prank was funny in the moment and making what some dismissed as merely a thoughtless outburst. Had PewDiePie still been an up-and-coming influencer, he might have ended his career with these incidents. As of 2022, however, he remained the number one YouTuber with over 100 million subscribers.

See **Lesson 6I: Coming Back for More**.

WHAT IS THE IMPACT OF INFLUENCERS ON TWEENS AND KIDS?

Teens and younger viewers love influencers.[11] In our own surveys of young internet users, words like *funny*, *entertaining*, and *informative*[12] were used to describe what they like best in influencers. While comedy was the biggest draw, too much *meanness*—to use the word most often used by tween respondents—was the biggest turnoff.

There is a special attractiveness of influencers for youth. Kids go from a narrow set of choices in elementary years to a much wider choice set in middle school. Today, middle schoolers face choices and issues that are different from previous generations due to a phenomenon known as **KGOY**, for "kids getting older, younger." This is not necessarily a bad thing, as kids get to see more diversity in their life choices and have more autonomy in how they self-identify. The challenge is that kids are still developmentally the same as before and may struggle with abstract ideas and having so many options. Too many choices can actually make a person less happy.[13]

For such youth, influencers can be guides in their choices. Influencers come across as experts in their fields, from gaming to fashion. Even more, they seem happy and successful after making their choices, so why shouldn't a fan follow and even imitate them? Making the influencer's choices the follower's can remove stressful decision points.[14] As an added bonus, following a particular influencer connects fans with like-minded people, thus giving them a group identity as members of the fan-tribe.

See **Lesson 6J: E Pluribus Unum**.

There are two general types of influencers that appeal to youth. The first kind are ones that intentionally target kids. Often, the influencers themselves are kids who promote toys and other kid-oriented products. Ryan Kaji began starring in YouTube videos around age four in 2015. Since then, *Ryan's World* has earned Ryan and his family over $25 million. What appeals to kids watching is less about particular toys than Ryan's joyful and happy attitude, according to his fans. In the child consumer's mind, Ryan's happiness then becomes connected to the toy, making the sponsors happy.

See **Lesson 6K: Peering at Peers**.

The other kind of influencer that youth watch might be called the accidental inspirers. These are usually influencers who are older, teens and twenty-somethings, who do not necessarily target youthful followers but attract them nevertheless. For kids, the attraction is **aspirational.** These influencers are famous, popular, and successful, everything that tweens hope to be. The influencers are **videogenic,** as they are relaxed on camera and move about with self-assured coolness.

See **Lesson 6L: You Can Be Anything** *We* **Want You to Be.**

Is there any harm in watching influencers, liking them, even following their suggestions, sways, or nudges? Usually not. Just as previous kids swore eternal allegiance to their idols and then eventually moved on, kids today will do so too. Most of us had a favorite celebrity that we followed when we were younger and eventually outgrew.

There are, however, two potential dangers to kids watching online influencers, even if they are essentially amplifications of what influencers have always done. First, influencer swaying is yet another vehicle for instilling over-consumerism into kids. The videos look like fun, but behind them are adults plotting how to use those videos to inculcate stealth messaging that a person needs to buy things to be seen as a person of value. Sufficiency is not the end goal—getting more is. It's not a fair game, as kids don't even realize they are playing it until their consumer habits and views—good, bad, and possibly disastrous—are inculcated.

The other danger is that influencers, especially the ones kids aspire to be, can have a profound effect as youth are discovering and forming their own identities. A rich variety of personalities make up the body of influencers, and most have the message that it is OK to be whoever you are or want to be. There still remains, however, some ingrained narrow cultural channels that present limited examples of diversity even among influencers.

See **Lesson 6M: Boys Will Be . . .?**

NOTES

1. Those inventors formed a company called Magnavox, meaning "great (or big) voice."

2. It was a truly ironic event, as Coolidge was famous for his quiet, anything-but-speaking nature. He was known as "Silent Cal."

3. Adolf Hitler, unfortunately, was also one of the first to tap into what became known as *führerprinzip*, or the "leader principle." If a person looks, acts, and sounds larger than life, bigger than everyone else, the audience will see him as a leader and be inclined to follow him.

4. It is very telling that at the Franklin Delano Roosevelt Memorial in Washington, DC, there are many quotes and depictions of FDR, but one statue simply shows a man listening to the radio. Unfortunately, FDR also knew that he could not reveal everything. He was afflicted with polio and so spent the second half of his adult life and most of his political career in a wheelchair. It did not affect his ability as president,

but with preconceptions and biases what they were, FDR restricted media broadcast or reporting of his condition.

5. A good contrast was in the 1990s marketing of, of all things, bricks in Dallas home-building. One company did an ad featuring Troy Aikman, quarterback of the three-time Super Bowl champion Cowboys, telling folks that one brand was the "official brick" of the Dallas Cowboys. Another ad by a rival company featured a plain folks woman saying "Sorry, number eight" and explaining she trusted Aikman for winning Super Bowls but not for choosing bricks.

6. If this sounds a bit contradictory, it is not a new contradiction. Teens who rebel against conformity often then coalesce into a unified, homogenous group to celebrate and support everyone's individuality and nonconformity, from hippies to goth.

7. Felix Kjellberg, who began his online career as a Swedish gamer and vlogger.

8. A top reason young consumers turn away from a product or spokesperson is the feeling that the pitch or person is phony or inauthentic, regardless of the product. It's also a reason youth prefer a more personal, niche-directed appeal rather than a "this is good for everyone" claim.

9. BeReal.

10. One example of mercenary faked authenticity is the rise of using nano-influencers to promote products or political opinions. In **astroturfing,** large organizations pay people with smaller followings, say a few thousand or tens of thousands, to create what seems like grassroots buzz about a product or a vicious rumor about a political opponent. The influencers either mention it themselves or use a combination of **bots** and **sock puppets** to make it seem like many are discussing the issue.

11. In this circumstance, we are focusing on entertainment influencers. Influencers regarding politics, finance, and other more adult topics are naturally more attractive to twentysomethings and older.

12. The last usually for gaming influencers.

13. Part of what causes the unhappiness is the increased anxiety and fear of making the wrong choice.

14. We surveyed eight- to thirteen-year-olds on a number of topics. In one question, we asked how much it would affect you if an influencer you liked recommended a product or brand. The most common response was that they would check out the recommended product or brand (34.1 percent), with another 9.1 percent saying they would probably choose the recommended product or brand over others; 27.3 percent said such a recommendation would probably or definitely not affect their choice.

Chapter 6 Accompanying Lessons

LESSON 6A: LOOK OF A LEADER

Focus of Exploration

Leadership appearance

Intro Questions/Thoughts for Students

Have you ever met someone who, before you even got to know them, seemed like a leader to you? What was it about them that made you think that?

Go to a place where you do not know people, such as a café. Can you pick out the leaders? How can you tell? What are the clues that make you think they are the leaders?

Activity

Look up movie posters or go to a theater and study the posters. Especially for movies you haven't seen yet, can you figure out who is the leader in the movie's plot? Who is the one who mainly drives the story and action? Who are the followers? If it is a team, how can you tell, and do some team members seem more the leaders than others?

Be sure to look at where the people are looking in the posters. Some look right at you. Others look at one person, often in the middle. Sometimes the one person is looking off and up, like they have a vision. Maybe they are holding a map, or the item everyone wants. What other clues do you see? Try to compare the leadership image in different types of movies, like a drama or action movie with a comedy.

After you have studied how leadership is depicted, make a poster for the movie that is about your life. You will be the focus and star of the movie, so make yourself the leader. You can also add taglines like in real movie posters that hint at leadership, like "Where he goes, adventure follows!"

Follow-Up Questions/Discussions

What are the common movie portrayals or traits of leadership? Do you think those traits are used in real life? Look at some posters for political candidates seeking office and other real-world leadership. Are they similar?

Are there different kinds of leaders and leadership styles? Some leaders are liked or are inspirational; others are forceful. Some do the will of their followers; others tell the followers what to do. What kind of leader are you for your poster?

You probably have been told to be a leader, but not everyone wants to be a leader and certainly not all of the time. Sometimes we want to be comfortable in the crowd. Some people prefer to be the sidekick, the wise adviser, or the comic relief. When is it OK, maybe even best, to let others have a turn being leaders?

Do leaders need immediate followers? Can they be leaders from a distance, or inspire and lead people later? Who are past or remote leaders that inspire you?

How does leadership look online? Is it similar to movies or IRL? Look for online leaders and see if the traits are the same as what you found already. Are there other traits?

LESSON 6B: THEATERS OF THE MIND

Focus of Exploration

Empathy with media consumers

Intro Questions/Thoughts for Students

When you see someone watching, listening, or otherwise enjoying media, do you imagine what the media they are enjoying is?

When you see someone doing what you like to do, do you feel a connection with them, like you know what they are feeling?

Activity

Find two pictures online. One is of a person, preferably a kid, long ago listening to the radio. The other picture should be of a more modern kid watching something online. If possible, choose a pic where what is being watched can't be seen.

For each picture, write a short story about what is going on. Who is the person? What are they listening to or watching? What are they thinking? What else is going on in their life?

Follow-Up Questions/Discussions

Did you make the two stories similar or different? If different, how so? Why?

Do you think kids in the past felt the same way using media as kids today? Was their entertainment similar? Why or why not?

Empathy is feeling a connection with someone as to what they are feeling in that moment. Do you feel a kind of connection with either or both kids in the picture? What kind of situations or activities have you seen someone doing where you felt empathy with what you imagined they were feeling?

LESSON 6C: INSIDE SCOOP

Focus of Exploration

False intimacy

Intro Questions/Thoughts for Students

Do you like to read about the private lives of famous or public people? Do you like to read about what they do when they are not in public? Why or why not?

Activity

Find online magazines that reveal the lives and opinions of celebrities that you and your friends like. Some, like *J-14*, *Seventeen*, and *Teen Vogue*, are written specifically for teen fans, while *People* and *Vogue* are for a general, more mature audience.

Look for patterns of topics covered. What are the most popular? How much do the celebrities reveal? How different are the teen-oriented magazines in their interviews and revelations from the general audience mags?

Follow-Up Questions/Discussions

Do you believe the interviews are genuine? Do some seem to be more like an ad or promotion for the celebrity than an investigation? Why would a celebrity reveal personal details or give their opinion? Is there a risk for them doing that? Are there any celebrities famous for not giving interviews or remaining private? How do you feel about that?

Why do you, as a fan, enjoy reading about the personal lives and opinions of celebrities? Have the articles ever made you like them less? If you found out the articles and interviews were not authentic, that the celebrity agreed to have his or her answers made up, would you think less of the celebrity or not? If a celebrity you liked a couple of years ago came out and said an interview was designed to have fans like them more, would you feel differently about them?

What is the difference, if you see any, between the teen magazines and the general audience magazines? Is there a difference in topics or depth? Is there ever anything really bad about celebrities in the teen ones? What about the general audience mags?

If the teen "revelation" magazines were part of a publicity system rather than honest, authentic reporting, would you want to know? Is there some fun to playing along with the fan fantasy of getting to know celebrities?

LESSON 6D: JUST LIKE YOU

Focus of Exploration

Celebrity connection by appearing as ordinary folks

Intro Questions/Thoughts for Students

Have you heard celebrities tell stories to say their lives are just like their fans'? Do celebrities talk about their struggles being similar to those of their fans? How do you feel when you hear that?

Activity

Look for interviews where celebrities describe their life, their concerns, or their challenges as similar to those of their fans or everyday people. Group the topics they bring up into categories, like relationships, mental or physical health, paying bills, work pressure, having free time, and other categories.

Also look for when celebrities go "natural" and show themselves being casual in dress, doing activities like cooking or chilling in their home. Again, try to see if there are patterns.

Follow-Up Questions/Discussions

There is no doubt that when a person is struggling, hearing that others struggle can help as they realize they are not alone. For you, does hearing about the similar struggles of celebrities help? What about hearing about similar struggles of ordinary people who are not celebrities? What about those of your friends?

What kind of topics and struggles did you hear about most often from celebrities? Were there any topics you did *not* hear about? If there were, was that because celebs don't have those struggles or the topic is too personal for them to discuss? If there is a topic you would like discussed, write to your favorite celeb and ask.

Was there a difference in the "just like you" messages between male and female celebrities? If so, why do you think that is?

Some issues, like personal insecurity, are common to both celebs and non-celebs. Some may be actually more of a challenge for celebrities, like privacy or wondering if people like them for themselves or because they are popular. Some may be more of a challenge for non-celebs. Celebrities often have personal trainers and dieticians who can help them with body goals, while most ordinary people do not. Do you think about that when hearing celebs talk of their struggles?

What is your opinion of celebs showing their "natural" looks or home or activities? If you found out that they had their hair and makeup done just before they told you they are "just waking up and must look awful," would you be bothered by inauthenticity? What about if their filmed playtime with their child was staged and they actually didn't do it that often? Is faking it just part of the celebrity game, especially with all the pressure to be on show for everyone? What kind of **posing** by celebrities would be too much for you? Do noncelebrities also pose like that?

What are the benefits for everyone in celebrities showing they are like noncelebrities? Does it give hope and encouragement to people? What are the possible downsides, like creating standards the ordinary person would find hard to meet? Overall, is it a good or bad thing in your view? Is it up to the fan to make it good or bad?

LESSON 6E: UNDER THE INFLUENCER

Focus of Exploration

Influencer advertising, product placement

Intro Questions/Thoughts for Students

Are you pretty good at recognizing ads, pitches, or pushes for you to buy something?

Have you ever tried to influence someone to choose or do something by casually mentioning it or even by showing it to them without directly mentioning it?

Think of a person whose videos you like to watch. Can you off the top of your head think of a product or brand you can associate with them? Maybe one they said they liked?

Activity

Watch a video posted by someone whose videos you like or by a famous **influencer**. Look for two kinds of brand pushes:

- Direct: A specific ad before, during, or after the content. Also, look if anyone in the video says anything to directly push something by saying it is a sponsor, or that you should check it out.
- Indirect: It's somewhere in the content but not directly pushed toward you. The product or brand could be mentioned in passing, like "I drank a Coke just before," or it is shown on-screen, like the people in the video are wearing it. If it has a distinctive shape or color that you can identify and you see that, it counts.

If you can, do this with a friend or family member and then see who caught the most pushes.

URL of video: _____
Name of influencer: _____
General topic of video: _____

For each push you see, try to mark down:

- The time in the video you saw the product pushed or shown.
- The brand or specific product pushed.

- If directly pushed, how was it done (specific ad or recommended by the person in the video)?
- If indirectly pushed, how was it done (casually mentioned, the person in the video interacts with it, or it is just there)?

Remember, a push isn't just for products. It can be for a service, a place, or even a person like another celebrity. Anything that gets you to think about checking it out or consuming it is a push.

Follow-Up Questions/Discussions

Were you better at finding direct or indirect ads, at least as compared with your friend? Why do you think that is?

Did you notice music in the background, or locations for the shots? They might be placements or ads as well, such as to visit that spot.

Most pushes are fly-bys, where the content mentions or shows it briefly and then the content moves on. Some are continuing, such as when the influencer repeatedly mentions it or discusses the brand a long time, or it remains in view a long time. Did you catch any of those?

Do you think such pushes work? Can seeing a push, maybe one you don't consciously notice, make you more likely to try something if it is by someone you like? Studies say yes. One push may not do the trick, but if they happen repeatedly over time, a viewer can be **swayed** to making it a regular choice, even a preference. Would you check out a brand if a favorite influencer recommended it? Are there any brands you think you have been swayed to try?

Besides promoting a product, can an influencer also be promoting themself? What is the benefit of promoting oneself, such as asking fans to watch or like their videos? How do people self-promote in the real world? Do you notice it when they do? Do you like it? Do *you* self-promote? When is it OK?

LESSON 6F: PAID TO BE AUTHENTIC

Focus of Exploration

Personal endorsements looking authentic, persona

Intro Questions/Thoughts for Students

What are the signs of someone being **authentic** or speaking from the heart? How can you tell when such speaking from the heart is real or not?

Do you like it when actors or influencers step "out of their **persona**" to share their personal, authentic selves with you? What about when they make personal endorsements of products or activities? Do those personal recommendations affect you?

If a person who recommends something is a celebrity, does that sway you more to try it than if they were a noncelebrity? Why or why not? Have you ever heard from friends or others about a famous personality or influencer asking people to do something? Did you feel like you wanted to check it out? Was it more because of the celebrity or your friends?

Activity

Look for public personalities such as actors, musicians, and influencers seeming to drop their public image to "speak from the heart" or purport to be authentic. Look for when they ask you to choose something, such as a product, activity, action, or cause.

As you find these moments, look for clues to judge their authenticity, such as using words like "for real," "honestly," or "this is me." See if they look right at you or look off in the distance. Is the presentation more casual, like they are dressed down and in their home? Does the casualness look real or staged?

Finally, consider what they are asking you to choose. Ask yourself if the personality has anything to gain by you doing what they ask, whether money or even popularity.

Follow-Up Questions/Discussions

Actors, influencers, and other public personalities have a persona, a public personality they project as part of their image, like a performance mask in ancient Greek theater. Sometimes the persona is similar to what the person is really like; sometimes it's different. Is there a way you can tell when a personality says they are taking off the persona mask that they are being authentic and not just showing a second mask?

It's hard to think of anything that doesn't benefit the person asking you to do something in some way. Even if they ask you to support a charity, the personality obviously wants that charity supported. So, how much benefit does the personality get before we can say it is not really "from the heart" or authentic? What about if the personality acquires fame or a reputation as a good person, increasing their number of likes, or they get talked about by you and friends with "Did you hear her say . . .?" When, for you, does it stop being authentic? If the charity benefits in any case, does it matter?

When a person asks you to do something "for them" or "because it's the right thing" but they also benefit—such as getting money or fame—it's called a *conflict of interest*. Should famous people and other influencers have to disclose if they have a stake or conflict of interest?

Being persuaded to try something by a celebrity isn't just for kids. Ask your parents to list adult celebrities who push products, brands, or choices. Ask your parents which celebrities they might listen to and for what products.

Do you have a persona? How is it the same and how is it different from the real you? When do you use it? How do you decide when to be authentic and when to use the persona? Is there a difference between your online persona and the authentic you?

LESSON 6G: MAKE YOUR OWN AUTHENTIC, NON-MADE, VIDEO

Focus of Exploration

Authenticity, social calculus

Intro Questions/Thoughts for Students

Have you ever pretended to be really interested or invested in something, to care a great deal, in order to get someone to like or do something? Was that OK? Would you be mad if someone did that to you? Under what circumstances?

Authenticity can be powerful, so much so that people are learning how to *look* authentic to get other people to buy and do things. Is that OK to do if you don't really mean it and are doing so to get what you want? When is it OK and when is it not OK?

Activity

Think of an ordinary thing in your house, like a mop or piece of furniture. Make a pretend social app video of about two minutes where you appear to promote it authentically. Tell a personal story of how the thing helped you or means so much in your life. Your goal is to push the thing so people will be interested in it but not make it look like an obvious sales push.

For added fun, make the video with a friend in which you two use a made-up word or phrase but make it seem totally natural, as if you have been using the word a long time. You can start to use the word in public—again, authentically and not pushing it—to see if others start using it in response to your soft sway.

Follow-Up Questions/Discussions

How hard was it to look authentic? It takes a lot of acting, but you can use techniques like looking off like you didn't even realize there was a camera—it was just you talking out loud. If so, where did you learn these ways to look authentic? If you are using them here, might others be using them in their videos to push you with fake authenticity? Look for some online.

It's hard to be on guard and have to always ask "Did they really mean it?" or "What did they really mean by saying that?" It's called **social calculus**, having to add up all the clues and then deciding what is the best way to respond. It's similar to when you have to decide if a compliment a person gave you was real or sarcasm. It's tiring because you have to be on guard and work extra hard to catch things when you want to just take things at face value. When should you be ready to do social calculus and when is it safe to just take things as they seem?

All of these subtle pushes, including trying to get people to use your made-up word, can influence people. If you push someone at a moment of decision, such as choosing your made-up word to use or buying the brand you recommended, it is called a **nudge**. If it happens long enough, the choice becomes a habit you don't even think about. Then all these pushes add up to being **sways**. You probably can't remember who first taught you to use "cool" as a word for something you like, but you heard it over time and now you choose that word without even thinking. Maybe your new word can sway people. Wouldn't that be cool?

LESSON 6H: HOW IS THE INTERNET CONNECTION?

Focus of Exploration

Connecting with influencers

Intro Questions/Thoughts for Students

When someone is connecting with what another person is saying, how is that shown? Do they lean in, smile, or nod? What are other signs?

When a person is speaking, how do they seem to reach out to connect with the audience? What are their body movements, facial expressions, and even words that they use to make a connection?

Activity

Go somewhere public where you can watch people, maybe a café or public hangout space. Watch people talk and look for ones that appear to be "connecting" or forming a bond with each other.

Write down what you see as the signs of connecting, especially by the speaker. Do they lean in or assume other body positions that imply they are connecting? If you can see their faces, what do their eyes focus on and for how long? Do they occasionally smile or nod as affirmation to each other? What else do you see?

Compare the clues you have seen with other speaker-audience groups that don't seem to be connecting. Do they have the same body and facial signs, or do they have different ones?

Now take all you learned IRL and watch videos online that feature an **influencer** speaking to their audience. Do you see the same signs of trying to connect? Do you see different signs or ways the influencer tries to connect?

Follow-Up Questions/Discussions

Even in our internet age, it is easier to connect with someone in person than online for most people. Why do you think that is? Do you think there will be a day when you connect as deeply online as in person?

There are challenges to making online connections, especially by way of one-way videos as opposed to two-way chatting. How do the influencers try to connect? Are they at a desk or more casual, such as lying down? What is the setting? Are the shots close-ups or from a distance? What are online techniques to make connections?

Connection also comes from the words. Someone who appears to be opening up or sharing personal information is making an offering to connect that is often accepted, even reciprocated. Do you see influencers doing that online? Sometimes informal speech makes more of a connection than using fancy, formal words. Do you see that in the videos?

What about two-way online connections by way of text? Is it hard to feel a connection because it is only words, or easy because the communication is two-way? Do you feel more connection from one-way video or two-way text? Is the reply to a text, "Yeah, me too," a connector for you? Does it depend if it is from a friend or a stranger?

One challenge for making connections is when one person is doing most or all of the communicating. Then, the speaker has to keep reinforcing the connection by acknowledging the listeners by thanking them, referring to them, and otherwise include them in the "conversation." Do influencers do this in their videos?

Some professionals, like teachers, pick up techniques for connecting and don't realize they are using them. Try to see how your teachers connect.

LESSON 6I: COMING BACK FOR MORE

Focus of Exploration

Captured audience, fan loyalty

Intro Questions/Thoughts for Students

Have you ever stopped watching a show you liked because the content stopped being entertaining? Did you stop at once, or did you give it a few more tries before you gave up? Why?

Are there any shows, entertainment, or influencers you feel loyal to? What would it take for you to stop being a fan?

Have you ever stopped being a fan of an entertainer or influencer because of something they did away from their show? Maybe some personal behavior or statement? How much do you think about the kind of person a celebrity is in deciding if you will watch their content?

Activity

For your favorite online celebrity, watch their videos for ways they try to get you coming back for more. These might include teasers about the next show or saying something will be continued. Even within a show, look for how often the celebrity mentions something is coming up later in that episode or video.

Now try to find an online celebrity or influencer who made the news for something bad they said or did. You may have to research first and then watch their videos. How did they respond? Did they talk about the bad thing? Did they apologize or offer a defense? Did they double down and say they did nothing wrong or attack their critics?

Follow-Up Questions/Discussions

Celebrities and their fans sometimes have a sort of social contract that as long as the celebrity entertains, the fan will be loyal. If the celebrity stops entertaining in the way the fan likes, the contract is broken and the fan leaves. Do you feel like you owe some celebrities your attention? Do you ever feel guilty or that you are letting them down by not taking in their latest content? On the other hand, do you feel you are free to stop following anytime you want?

Have you ever waited for some part that a celebrity teased or promised would be great and then you were disappointed by it? Did that affect your side of the celebrity/fan social contract?

When you are a loyal fan, what kind of negative news about the celebrity might cause you to break off your loyalty, even if the content was still good? Can you separate what the celebrity does or says from the entertainment and just enjoy their content? If you read that the celebrity did what you consider a good thing away from their entertainment, does that increase your loyalty to their content?

More than the social contract with celebrities, we all make unspoken social contracts with our friends and families. What are your expectations of your friends that are part of that social contract that you will do things for each other?

How do you feel watching a celebrity respond to bad reports about them? Do you judge their response the same way you would judge a friend responding to a bad report about them?

LESSON 6J: E PLURIBUS UNUM

Focus of Exploration

Power and draw of group unity in fandom

Intro Questions/Thoughts for Students

Is there a group or organization you feel very attached to? Do you feel like you draw power, support, or confidence just from being a member? Do you like being part of a group identity? Why?

What are the groups you belong to that have such things, such as your school?

Activity

Many online fan groups of celebrities have names for themselves beyond "Fans of . . ."[1] So, for a group you belong to like your family or group of friends or people you meet with who have a common interest who don't already have one, create everything a fan group needs:

- A catchy name, more than "Fans of . . ." or your family's last name
- A logo or mascot
- A unique word or sign that is only used within the group

Follow-Up Questions/Discussions

Why do you think groups and organizations, including even your school or club, give themselves a group name and adopt symbols and logos? Does it give you a greater sense of group identity? How so? Is this just as true for online groups?

If someone makes fun of the name or practices of your group, do you take it personally? Is it OK to make fun of another group's name or customs that you don't belong to?

The idea of bonding with a name or motto is not limited to young people and fandom. Adults do it and with serious things like politics. In fact, the title of this exercise comes from the phrase "e pluribus unum," a famous motto for a unified group. Do you know where that motto comes from? What other adult groups have names and symbols for unity?

---

1. You can see lists of them at https://popcrush.com/fan-nicknames-beliebers-directioners-swifties-list and https://en.wikipedia.org/wiki/List_of_fandom_names.

Is it OK for people to have different levels of commitment to a celebrity or cause but still be part of the group? Are there some groups you are a member of that you enjoy participating in but don't want to go all in with the names and customs? Has another member of that group given you grief for not being more into it?

LESSON 6K: PEERING AT PEERS

Focus of Exploration

Peer influencing versus aspirational influencing

Intro Questions/Thoughts for Students

When you watch videos online, for what kind of videos or topics do you like to watch content by people older than you, say more than three years? For what content would you prefer videos by someone about your same age?

Does it feel different getting advice or tips from someone your age versus someone older? What about a bit older, like more than three years? Do you feel embarrassed watching videos or getting tips from certain age-groups on certain topics? Which topics? Why?

Activity

Watch a video by a content provider or influencer your age. As you watch, try to go *meta*, which means you both watch the video and watch yourself. Ask yourself how you feel watching the video. Would you be embarrassed if your family saw you watching a video of someone your age? What about if friends saw you?

Also ask yourself how you feel about the person in the video who is about your age. Do you feel a connection with them? Is it similar to hearing from a friend? Why or why not?

Next, find a video on the same topic made by someone at least three years older than you. Watch it, go meta, and compare your feelings to the same-age content provider. Does it feel the same or different?

Follow-Up Questions/Discussions

Can you explain the difference in your feelings watching a content provider your age versus watching someone older? What are the advantages of each? A peer might know what you are going through right now, whereas older people can share experience. When is each better?

Part of the reason many prefer to watch older content providers, especially as they get a little older, is for **aspirational** purposes. They want to be older and act older, so they watch and imitate older people. When is that OK? When might it still be better to look at and consider what others your age are doing?

Ironically, adults sometimes intentionally seek guidance from younger people for things like the latest trends. Ask your parents what they would consult younger content providers about. Does their acting young ever embarrass you? Why?

LESSON 6L: YOU CAN BE ANYTHING *WE* WANT YOU TO BE

Focus of Exploration

Sways on children, using aspirational desires

Intro Questions/Thoughts for Students

Often, using a product means a change in your life, hopefully for the better. What is something you chose in order to change who you are or your whole life for the better? Did it work? Why or why not?

For something you tried to change with yourself or your life, how did you get the idea it would change things? Was it from a friend? From an advertisement? Did you discover it on your own?

Activity

Think of a product you are not currently using or an activity you are not already doing. Pretend to be checking it out. Look at the ads or comments as to what the advertisers and others say about it. Look especially for promises that the product or activity will not just help you or be fun but will change you or your life.

Are the ways they say it will change you or your life specific or general? Do they promise anything or maybe imply it, like having people in the ad more attracted to the product user? Do they **hedge** their promises, such as saying you could lose up to 1,000 pounds in a week but then say in small type "Results not guaranteed"?

Now watch your favorite content providers and influencers. Do they push or mention products or things that will make you a "new you" or change your life dramatically? Are they like the ads in their pushes, implications, and even hedges?

Follow-Up Questions/Discussions

Do you see any particular areas, such as health or looks, that people seem to want to change more? Is that a good thing? Most permanent changes take time and a lot of continuous effort. Do the ads say that? Do they send a different message? Why?

Focus on messaging that pushes changing your look. Do they imply or even say that changing your look changes who you are on the inside, or that it will completely change your life? Do you agree? Are the looks-changing pushes equally for males and females?

Look for any ads or statements that say you are OK just the way you are. Are there as many that have the "you're OK" message as ads that say to change? Why do you think that is?

Are the change-who-you-are messages online the same as those IRL? If you think there are more or fewer, why do you think that is? Online, there are not just videos and ads, but people can read comments, either in chat apps or in comments to videos. Do the comments also send messages to change who you are? How?

Can something **sway** you to change without even saying anything, such as a picture that you then compare yourself with? Can many such pictures constantly displayed over time become a long-term sway? How is that good and bad?

Once we get an idea that change is the key to happiness, can we get in the impulsive habit to keep looking for an upgrade? When might it be better to be happy with who one is and what one has, having enough, than looking for more? Is more always better?

Do **influencers** use the same language or techniques to tell you how you can be "better" or have more of something? Do you think they are advertising or profiting by their messaging? Should you consider that when hearing their message?

Influencers often tell you about a new product or change that made their life better. Is that the same as a friend telling you the same thing? When would you believe an influencer more, and when more a friend? If you found out a friend recommended something because they benefited from you changing, would that make you mad? What about if an influencer did that?

LESSON 6M: BOYS WILL BE . . .?

Focus of Exploration

Gender differences in influencer role models

Intro Questions/Thoughts for Students

For whichever gender you identify as, do you look to others of your gender for how you should act or what you should like? Do you ever disagree or decide you like something else?

If a person who identifies as a gender different from yours does or promotes something, do you consider it as much as if it were promoted by someone with the same gender identification as you? Why or why not?

Activity

Try to watch at least five videos by **influencers** who identify with the same gender as you do and then five by people who identify with another gender. It is important here that unless the content provider has specifically said what gender they identify as, you are making a guess by cultural clues that may or may not be how the person feels inside.

For what you perceive as male and female content providers, write out what are the most common topics each group discusses. It could be gaming, sports, fashion, makeup, or a mix, but look for topics that seem much more the focus of one gender group than another.

Also, look at the style of each gender group as a whole. Does one use humor more than the other? Is there a difference in communication, such as forceful or softer language, or hand and body movements? When they talk about gender, what words do they use, such as *man* versus *boy* or *woman* versus *girl*?

Follow-Up Questions/Discussions

This is not a scientific study. It is meant to get an impression, so that means there are "holes" in the data collection. We always worry about **sample size**. Also, you are intentionally looking for clues, and that differs from how you normally take in videos. You also have your own preconceptions and assumptions. So, it is always better to ask others for their perspectives on the same material as well.

What similarities did you see? What things do male and female influencers both do, or what topics do they discuss roughly equally? Which things were different?

Of course, if you find differences, the big question is *why* are there differences? Where do they come from? Do you think the differences online are similar to the differences in real life? Why or why not?

For the gender you identify as, did you feel a stronger interest, even connection or **affinity**, with the influencers who were the same gender as you? Why do you think that is? Is it only common interests or something more? Do you feel as comfortable watching influencers of another gender? Why or why not?

No doubt many differences between male and female influencers are a result of culture that sends a message that boys should be interested in certain things and act one way, girls another. Can the influencers, in turn, be showing how they were influenced? Do you think boys and girls imitate them and act in a similar way at least in part because of the messaging?

Chapter Seven

The Parasocial Relationship

Magnets were long seen as a kind of magic. That two metal objects can cause each other to move closer or farther away mystified people for centuries. There was clearly an invisible force at work. Humans played with the force, used it, even created it for centuries without understanding where the force came from or how it worked.

Understanding came in the early 1800s as scientists discovered the connection between magnetism and electricity, leading to Hans Christian Oersted's 1820 discovery of magnetic fields. People were now looking for other invisible fields of influence between objects, trying to quantify and tap into the power.

Almost fifty years before Oersted's breakthrough, Franz Mesmer looked for influential fields between humans. He came up with the theory that animals, including humans, had a mysterious fluid in their body that responded to magnets. He believed that placing magnets, along with his own presence that somehow boosted the force, could cure ailments. It also could induce a trancelike state in which Mesmer could guide and influence a person. Mesmer called this bodily power to influence others *animal magnetism*.[1]

Putting people in a trance and influencing them came to be called *mesmerism*. The practice evolved and was renamed *hypnosis*. Scientists and doctors, including Sigmund Freud, explored its usage in treating patients. There was also concern about how it could be misused or even abused. In 1894, the novel *Trilby* both captured and intensified the concern. In the story, a young, innocent girl falls under the spell of a man named Svengali.[2] Svengali mesmerizes the girl, seduces her, and makes her dependent upon him as he makes her into a great singer.

The novel has faded from public memory, but the term *Svengali* and the idea it represents have not. *Svengali* now denotes a person who exerts his will on someone else, usually a naive or inexperienced person.[3] His will is almost never to do good.[4] The weakness of Svengali's power was that he had to be in close, regular proximity to his human puppet to reinforce his control. So, keeping the victim apart and at a distance from the Svengali could break the spell.

And then along came the internet . . .

See **Lesson 7A: UBU!**

We will come back to Svengali later, but let's first go back to something brought up in chapter 5, when we discussed how social networks, particularly Facebook, changed the meaning of *friend* from a person one feels close to and shares common interests with to also mean a person with whom one has linked social media accounts. Most people do not confuse the two; they don't consider someone with a linked account but whom they hardly know to be a true friend.

That's because the basic concept of *friendship* has not changed, even if it is hard to define. A person can probably name people who are their real friends, make a list of some of the things those friends do—and would not do—on their behalf, but still struggle to think of a precise definition of what *friendship* is. There would seem some basic, commonsense requirements, like that two people who are true friends actually know each other at least somewhat, if not well. Friends also each put something into the friendship, and both make efforts to keep it going. Friendship is not one-way.

Friendship is just one kind of **social relationship**. The *Encyclopedia of Social Medicine* uses this phrase to refer to "the connections that exist between people who have recurring interactions that are perceived by the participants to have personal meaning."[5] There are thus two components: connections between people and interaction meaningful to both.

Outside of social relationships are **incidental relationships**, where we see people perhaps briefly or one time, like a sales clerk at the store. There are also **formal relationships** such as with a doctor or teacher. There is even a hazy, gray area just outside of social relationships called **acquaintances**, who are people we know somewhat, interact with occasionally, but with whom we don't feel a personal connection like we do with social relationships. This could include a person you see at school or work that you say hi to but don't know too much about.

It's complicated. Some people might be in more than one category at the same time, like someone you work with on a project or team (formal), but outside of that is also a personal friend (social). Some people move between one group or another over time.

When making a decision, which ones should a person go to for advice? If it was something personal, someone with whom you have a social relationship is probably best. If you want an expert or an objective opinion, you might ask someone you have an incidental relationship with, like a clerk in a store, or a formal relationship with, like your doctor.

This complicated network of friends and different go-to's for advice has existed as long as humankind, but today it has gotten even more complicated because of . . . drumroll . . . the internet. In the old days, BC—as in *before computers*—people's networks, social and otherwise, were pretty much limited to individuals they knew personally, as in face-to-face.[6] There were some special cases, like a pen pal one wrote to, but for the most part an essential part of friendship was presence. Virtual friendships were "till we meet again."

Today, we have access to thousands of people through videos, social media, gaming rooms, and other manner of distant connections. You can instantly find a community of people with your same interests to chat about things like the news, your favorite band, or the "Easter eggs" hidden in your favorite game. From those common interests, incidental relationships and acquaintances can become social relationships, even close friendships, as people's common interests lead them to talk first about those interests, then other interests, and then about themselves and their lives. It's called an **affinity**, defined as liking someone, even having an attraction, based on having something in common with them.

Both in the online world and IRL, most of the above works the same. Relationships are based on connection, and youth today are comfortable making those connections from afar. Chatting and sharing lives through text is nearly the same for them as doing it in person, sometimes even preferred. As long as they both put effort and energy into the relationship, and those connections have meaning for both parties, who's to say it's any less of a friendship because they are not physically near? In any case, many, if not most, of today's social relationships for youth are hybrids, conducted and perpetuated both online and IRL.

One kind of relationship that has become prominent recently is the **parasocial relationship**. It's not new, but the internet has taken it to a new level. In a parasocial relationship, someone, let's say a typical kid, finds videos posted by an influencer online. The videos are appealing, as the content creator is funny, smart, maybe even good-looking. The influencer says things that appeal to the kid; perhaps they have a common interest, or the poster has good advice. In many ways, the poster seems to have more in common with the kid viewer than many of the kid's real-life friends and schoolmates. The youth starts to feel an affinity for the poster.

From watching more videos, maybe researching the influencer's background, the kid feels like he or she knows a lot about the influencer and starts imagining what the influencer is like off camera. Unaware of **personas**,[7] inexperienced viewers assume the influencer is the same off camera as on. The fan starts to create a whole, but largely imagined, concept of the influencer, like a 3-D printer. He or she starts to feel a friendship. The fan accepts suggestions, leads, and any advice the influencer broadcasts because the fan now considers the influencer a known and trusted *friend* in a personal, not Facebook, sense.

Why would someone go so all in for a one-way relationship? It's complicated. What we can say is that tweens and other youth look for a tribe to join as part of discovering their self-identity. In searching for a tribe, youth often fixate on a supposed leader as defining the tribe and giving it an identity they can connect with. As we said before, parasocial relationships are not new in the sense that youth have had them going back generations.[8] There were rabid fans of the Beatles, before them Frank Sinatra, and before him Rudy Vallee. Movie stars, sports figures, and other celebrities often were solicited for advice from youth looking for guidance.[9]

What is new about parasocial relationships is how the internet creates an illusion of intimacy that magnifies the intensity of the attraction. Most youth don't form parasocial relationships, but there are the kids for whom typical youth awkwardness feels even greater. They feel like a square peg in a culture of round holes and they don't have, for many reasons, an adequate social support system. In the privacy of their room, however, they find online a person whose interests, words, and outlook speak to them.

We also have to remember that seeking out help or guidance begins with trust. A young person may have a concern or question, and their school may have a counselor, but if no trust relationship has been previously established, it could be difficult for the child to come forward.[10]

On the other hand, the isolated youth sees an online or social media poster who shares common interests and has an inviting manner, the first elements that a trust relationship is built on. It goes from there. Fans may post comments to videos or send notes, and through that feel like a connection is being made. That the connection is not two-way, person-to-person can actually be an upside. The awkward-feeling fan doesn't have to worry about saying the wrong thing or being rejected, hiding in the safety of a one-way relationship. They can imagine with all positivity what the influencer would say if they could directly interact.

See **Lesson 7B: Lifelines**.

The parasocial relationship could be called a cyber-Svengali one. The fan is enthralled by the online persona and will follow them, even against the advice of other people in his or her life. The illusion of intimacy reinforces the attraction.[11] In one sense, however, the circumstances of attraction are different from before. With the traditional Svengali, it is the person in power who reaches out to the follower and enwraps him or her in their dominating magnetic field. With a parasocial relationship, the power person may be broadcasting, but it is to the general world. The follower comes to them, led to the attractive field by the circumstances in his or her life.

This makes all the difference in deciding how to address the circumstance. Blaming the Svengali-influencer, even disconnecting the follower from them, may not solve the problem. The follower could continue to be swayed by the circumstances of his or her life to just find another persona with which to form a parasocial relationship. There are plenty out there.

Those outside of the parasocial relationship can see that it is only a one-way connection. Friends are aware of each other and *both* put effort into the relationship and *both* get something out of it. In a parasocial relationship, the influencer isn't putting anything into the specific relationship with that follower. For the most part, the influencer doesn't even know the viewer exists. They thank everyone for their support, saying they couldn't do what they do without support and feedback from viewers "like you." The influencer reads and acknowledges some comments, even from the very viewer who feels the friendship, but it still is pretty much a one-way thing.

Most followers grow out of parasocial relationships, just as rabid fans in years past moved on to new idols and then to other things. Most obsessions of youth fade by teen years, and teen idols lose their appeal as their fans enter adulthood, get jobs, and get married. Problems can obstruct this typical exit path, however.

If the viewer gets too wrapped up, overzealous, even fanatical, he or she can lose balance. The internet experience, especially if done alone in one's room, can disconnect the fan from real-life influences and become extremely intense. An overzealous or excessive fan is called a **stan**.[12] The internet has been identified repeatedly as a place that can create "stan culture."[13]

See **Lesson 7C: Stan by Me**.

If taken to the extreme, two potential problems have been seen happening with stans created by parasocial relationships. First, the stan sees only one way, their influencer's way, of doing life. Anything else or different becomes wrong, even a threat. Because the follower feels too connected to their idol, critics of the influencer are seen as critics of the follower. It's great to be a loyal fan, but viewers need to remember that we all can like, and dislike, different things. It's OK to not like what someone else loves. It's also true that just because you may not like something someone else loves, that doesn't mean you don't like *them*.[14]

Some stans, however, take criticism of their favorite influencers personally. They rally together to say they won't let their idol be bullied. Ironically, they then become a bullying mob against people who just have different tastes. Some of the pushback tricks can be amusing at first, but it can go too far and cost others time and money, even their safety, just because they had another opinion.

See **Lesson 7D: Stan Your Ground**.

The other danger of living in stan culture is the possible isolation from other aspects of life, including the real world. Real life is tricky. It's hard to interact with others because you don't have complete control of the situation. It's risky and scary to put oneself out there. It takes effort. For tweens, most of their challenges feel intense, but they often are comparatively small and help build fortitude and coping strategies for bigger challenges they will face as adults.

A stan, however, avoids those training challenges by seeking refuge in their room with their influencer. The viewer doesn't have to worry about taking risks and being embarrassed or other negative emotions. Some viewers start choosing the influencer over other options, including even real-life friends. This creates a disconnect which reinforces the awkward person's discomfort and causes them to seek further refuge.

The vicious spiral can go unchecked. Real-life interaction is riskier and messier, but the rewards are far greater, including actual friendship or even just the acknowledgment that you are a living, breathing human being of value. Increased isolation can lead to anxiety, depression, and other problems.[15]

See **Lesson 7E: Balancing Act**.

NOTES

1. Today, *animal magnetism* denotes a person's wordless attractiveness, often sexual, by their mere presence.

2. Unfortunately, Svengali is portrayed and referenced using very anti-Semitic tropes of the time.

3. The usual portrayal is of a male dominating a weak-willed and pliable female, born in part out of sexist notions of the genders.

4. The *Svengali defense* in law is when someone accused of misdeeds claims they did so because they were under the influence of an overpowering mastermind who compelled them to act.

5. Kristin J. August and Karen S. Rook, "Social Relationships," in *Encyclopedia of Behavioral Medicine* (New York: Springer, 2013), 1838–42, https://doi.org/10.1007/978-1-4419-1005-9_59.

6. Even in disliking people, philosophers and psychologists believed that one could dislike the idea of a person, such as a stereotype or generalization about them, from afar but that true dislike could only come from personally knowing the other person.

7. The fan only thinks of the celebrity in this one dimension of how they present themselves online. Combined with their added imagining, the fan will reject, even angrily, any reports that go against the persona, such as celebrity gossip articles or friends criticizing the influencer.

8. The term *parasocial relationship* was coined in 1956. Donald Horton and Richard Wohl, "Mass Communication and Para-Social Interaction," *Psychiatry* 19, no. 3 (August 1956): 215–29, https://doi.org/10.1080/00332747.1956.11023049.

9. John Lodge was a member of the very popular 1970s band the Moody Blues. The band was known for songs with mystical lyrics that fans studied for secret messages. According to Lodge, he came home from a tour to find a swarm of fans camped on his front garden, telling him he was going to "save the Earth." This inspired Lodge to write the song "I'm Just a Singer (in a Rock and Roll Band)." The song became a hit that fans then studied for more secret messages.

10. This is in no way a criticism of school counselors. They are wonderful assets to school communities, but they are overworked and overburdened. They cannot form a preexisting trust relationship with every child in their community.

11. An example of **fake intimacy** is when an influencer posts a video of themselves lying in their bedroom, using a stage-whisper voice, to give the feeling that the viewer is being let into the restricted area and being told information not meant for everyone to hear.

12. The word traces back to a 2000 song by Eminem about a fan who is driven over the edge when Eminem does not reply to his fan mail.

13. See Maya Nelson, "The Dark Side of Stan Culture," *Stanford Daily*, August 24, 2021, https://stanforddaily.com/2021/08/23/the-dark-side-of-stan-culture.

14. Unfortunately, this stan-like view has come into adult politics, where people with opposing views are not seen as wanting a different approach to make society better, but as enemies bent on destroying society. This has made reconciliation, such as after an election, problematic.

15. See Peng Sha and Xiaoyu Dong, "Research on Adolescents Regarding the Indirect Effect of Depression, Anxiety, and Stress between TikTok Use Disorder and Memory Loss," *International Journal of Environmental Research and Public Health* 18, no. 16 (August 21, 2021): 8820, https://doi.org/10.3390/ijerph18168820.

Chapter 7 Accompanying Lessons

LESSON 7A: UBU!

Focus of Exploration

Self-awareness, fiction as a way to understanding

Intro Questions/Thoughts for Students

Have you ever met someone that reminded you of a character in a story? Once you thought of it, did you start to see the person in terms of that character in other ways?

Activity

One of the many reasons fiction is great is that we get to meet different personalities and characters that we wouldn't normally meet in real life. As made up as the characters are, the best ones still have traits we see in real people. Harry Potter is a determined outsider. Count Olaf is a sinister older person taking advantage of young people. Even Goldilocks is just an unaware person getting deeper into trouble. We then see people we really know with similar traits.

Imagine your life were a novel and you are the main character. Of course, your story is widely popular, so much so that people tell others "You are such a [your name]!" because they are like you in how they act or what they think.

Write out what that would mean. What would a typical character based on you do or think? You can even write a fantasy or adventure story with you and some friends as other characters in which you respond to crazy circumstances in your typical way.

After you write your story, have your parents or friends read it. Change the name of the character that is based on you to a name different from your own and see if they pick up that the character is you. You can also incorporate how you see them, though you should be careful so as not to offend them.

Follow-Up Questions/Discussions

You probably had a lot of material to work with to create your character based on what you do in real life. How about if you now made a character based on your online self? Would it be more secretive or more outgoing and adventurous? More chatty or more mysterious? Can you write a story that takes place mainly online that includes your internet you?

If you don't like the way your character is turning out, why is that? Is it that you don't think the character is a good depiction of you? Maybe you don't like the part of you depicted by the character? If it is the character, rewrite it. If it is you, you may have to ask someone what they think of that part of you that you don't like. Often, what we don't like about ourselves is something other people love about us, including personality or even looks. We also change over time, so who you are now won't be the same character you will be in a couple of years, just like how characters in a book series grow and change.

LESSON 7B: LIFELINES

Focus of Exploration

Resources for guidance

Intro Questions/Thoughts for Students

When you are picking someone to seek advice from, what do you consider? You want someone you can trust and is smart, but what other factors are important?

Activity

If you have a problem, situation, or concern you would like guidance on, think of someone you know in real life you could consult and someone online who might give you advice. For each of them, rank them 1 (low) to 5 (high) in the following categories:

- Seems knowledgeable in that problem, like an expert.
- Has been in a similar situation so has experience.
- Knows you personally and can give an answer tailored to your life.
- You trust them to be confidential and caring.
- Availability and speed to hear your problem and get back an answer.
- You won't be embarrassed for them to know about your problem.

Total up the score and see who has the highest total. Consider them for helping.

Follow-Up Questions/Discussions

Depending on the concern or problem, some categories might be more important than others. Can you weigh them differently to account for that?

Speed of hearing and replying might seem like an odd factor, but some problems need to be addressed soon. Some people are wise but busy. Try writing out a short note asking for advice, like writing to an advice column. Send it to some people, like a trusted friend, a school counselor, and an online personality. See how fast they respond.

Some of the categories, like expertise, are more about the person you are looking to. Others, like your embarrassment, are more about how you feel. Seeking and getting advice is a two-way event, and you have to have both parties be into it.

There is one person who should rank high in most of these categories that you might forget: yourself. You may not have the expertise or experience, but you care about yourself and probably know more than you think. It may sound silly, but write a letter asking yourself for advice. Wait a few days and then answer the letter. You might have enough hindsight to give yourself good advice!

LESSON 7C: STAN BY ME

Focus of Exploration

Stans, captured consumer

Intro Questions/Thoughts for Students

You often hear people say they are "obsessed with" or completely "devoted to" choosing something, even for something like a drink. What choices do you feel that way about?

Think about a time you were completely into or always chose one thing, but then changed. What made you change? Was it a sudden change, or did it happen slowly over time? Was there an outside reason, or was the change from inside you?

Once you have dropped something you always chose, did you ever go back to choosing it? If you did go back, was it with the same intensity and joy in choosing it? Why or why not?

Activity

Think of two things that you always choose to do or experience. It can be a food or clothing style that you are "obsessed with" or "can't live without." Maybe it's an activity you won't turn down, like going to a certain place.

For each thing, write the reasons why you first came to always choose that one thing. Then, write out if those reasons still exist and whether they are still that strong. Are there any negatives, old or new, to doing it still? Finally, think of alternatives or substitutes and see if there is one you should try just to compare. If there is nothing, write out the reasons why nothing can compare, and stick with your choice!

If neither of your two things is something you experience or do online, do the activity for a third thing that you always choose to do online.

Follow-Up Questions/Discussions

Is there any harm in being completely and exclusively devoted to something? When is it OK to like something but not be totally devoted to it? If it's a celebrity a person unquestionably chooses and supports, it's called being a **stan**.

When we say we are a devoted fan of a celebrity, how can we know if we are a fan of their product (their music or other talent) or them personally? Can you separate the two? Is it OK to be a fan of what they do but not care so much about them personally?

Why do some people go all in and become stans and others do not, even if they both like the same thing? People approaching stan fandom don't see it as too much, but others might. Think of a celebrity you don't particularly like and look for how stans of that celebrity behave. What behaviors do you see? Have you ever acted like that toward a celebrity? Would you know when you were approaching being a stan?

People don't always want to think about possible alternatives to things they are devoted to. Why do you think that is? It's sometimes easier to choose one thing and then be all in on it. Is there any harm to rethinking about things one has been committed to for a long time? Is there anything for you that has become a fixed choice, a **sway**, that should not be reexamined?

LESSON 7D: STAN YOUR GROUND

Focus of Exploration

Positive support as a fan, othering

Intro Questions/Thoughts for Students

What does it mean to take something personally? When someone says they don't like something you did, or something you like, do you ever feel like it is a criticism of you? Why?

If a person does something you don't like, not because you think it's wrong but because it's not your taste, do you judge the other person? Do you think less of them? Why or why not?

Activity

Think of things and celebrities you really like a lot. If you can, think of things that are the only things you will do or consume of that category. You might have one kind of soda you will drink, or only one sport you will play or be a fan of, or one music group you will listen to.

For that thing, activity, or celebrity, think of alternatives someone else might choose. Try to think of someone who does prefer that alternative, maybe even a friend.

Now, here's the tricky part. For that person, think of other things you have in common with them. Maybe you both share the same taste in clothes or comedies? Maybe at one time you were both devoted fans of the same thing? Draw a Venn diagram of your tastes.

Follow-Up Questions/Discussions

Sports teams compete, and we say some are rivals, but even in the highest stakes game, they shake hands afterward and even are friends off the pitch or court. Why is that? Do their fans act the same way?

How can we take disagreement or criticism of what we like personally but not take it as criticism of ourselves? Perhaps we can at that moment think of a friend who has different tastes but whom we still like. Could that remind us that the person disagreeing with our taste is still like us? If someone does try to say you are not good because they don't like your taste, what can you do? Does their opinion of what you like matter to you? Should it?

One of the reasons we start to not like others who have different tastes or preferences is because of **othering**. We tend to hang around with people who like the same things. People who like different things are often not in front of us. They become less individuals and more a mass of people who are rivals. Pretty soon, we think of them as a dark mass of "others." At that point, we stop thinking of them as having feelings like ours. We start to put them down and even do hurtful things to them that we would never think of doing if they were standing in front of us. Are there situations when you have seen othering, where people who are different were grouped and criticized simply for being different? What can you do when you see it happen?

Othering is, unfortunately, common on the internet, especially in comments. Why do you think that is? If the comments build and build, they can lead to bullying, harassment, and actual acts. What can you do when you see othering start online?

Another problem with differences online is that it is hard to see the "too far" line. Something may start as good-natured teasing. Face-to-face, you can see in a person's face when it may be going too far. You can't do so online. Also, in real life there are often just a couple of people involved so it is easier to control or stop things before they go too far. Online, many people can weigh in, and it only takes one to take it too far. How can we keep better control of jokes and teasing online to keep it good-natured without getting out of hand?

LESSON 7E: BALANCING ACT

Focus of Exploration

How to express concern for others who appear out of balance in fandom

Intro Questions/Thoughts for Students

If you saw a friend making what you considered unhealthy choices, what might you do? Would you talk to them? Would you let someone, like a parent or counselor, know?

It's important to have a good balance in life, especially between doing things alone and with others, focusing on work versus play, and online versus in real life. What might be the signs that a friend is out of balance in any of these ways that might be unhealthy?

Activity

In a group with friends, talk about and come up with warning signs that someone is trending toward an unhealthy balance in their life. Focus on these three balances:

- Spending time alone versus being with others
- Focusing on work and being productive versus relaxing and de-stressing
- Being engaged online versus in real life

Can you agree that you will let each other know if they see anyone give off warning signs that their choices are out of balance? You should also talk with helpful adults, such as school counselors, to let them know if you see the signs.

Follow-Up Questions/Discussions

For every balance, there is a range. Everyone has different comfort spots in this range. Some people like to be alone more than others or be online more, and that's OK. How can you tell when someone is more than just different, that their balance might be unhealthy? We all have times when the balance is off, like when a big school project is due and you have to give up some leisure time. One clue is whether the balance is restored after the situation is over. What might be other signs that there might be a problem?

What would you say if your friends expressed concern to you that something in your life was out of balance? Would you be angry? Would you appreciate their concern? Would you be willing to listen and think about your situation from their point of view?

You all probably are fans of people and activities online, but what are the signs that someone is too into that online person or activity, to the point of it being unhealthy? How does a person who is following an online personality in an unhealthy way talk about the celebrity? Are they open to different tastes or criticism, or are they hostile? Do they only talk about that celebrity or make all their decisions by what they think the celebrity would do? If someone you knew acted like this, what could you do?

Afterword

When the unfiltered data dump burst through our computer screens in the 1990s, we, the leading consumer society, were not prepared to consume it all. The creation of the online world inundated people with its wave of information and opinions from a thousand points of view. We had been acculturated to receiving information mostly in bite sizes from friends, neighbors, and filtered news sources. We had to adjust on the fly, sometimes not well enough.

Successive generations have become more accustomed to the online world. Today, thirty years after the internet first went public, fifteen years after carrying the internet in your pocket via a smartphone became ubiquitous, Gen A are the latest entrants into dual-world living. Born in the 2010s and later, they have grown up discovering both the real world and the online world simultaneously. They don't see the internet and real world as alternative realms, but as two parts of one larger universe for them.

We can give Gen A what we, the first internet users, did not have: pretraining and education in how to navigate and even thrive in facing the onslaught of online information and messaging. We can inform them about the nudges and sways that exist online, to make them more resistant to passively and subconsciously absorbing the messages and values as their own without first asking, "Do I want this to be part of me?" Youth can be educated to become active consumers who control their information diet just as they are similarly learning how to choose healthy food for their body. We can empower them to know they have a choice.

The online world seemingly has the power to inform us, entertain us, and even tell us who we are and should be. Perhaps, then, the most important message we can instill in Gen A, and everyone who spends time online, is that the *internet* actually does none of these. It is merely a tool, like a hammer. The internet is not sentient, and like any tool, can be used for good or bad, to help or harm. The real power is in the user.

Youth should be taught that rather than they needing the internet, the internet needs them far more. When it comes to power, even the youngest users, ironically, have a power that the internet doesn't have, and to many marketers' frustration can't be bought. It's free and limitless and inside every person.

The power of choice.

Please use it abundantly and wisely.

Glossary

acquaintance: Someone we have interactions with on a semi-regular basis but with whom we don't have enough *affinity* to consider them a friend.
affinity: Liking someone, even having an attraction to them, based on having something in common with them.
algorithm: A set of rules or guiding instructions put into programs and other processes to guide how they carry out their operations.
aspirational motivation: Making choices in order to imitate or follow the example of celebrities or individuals a person admires. Often inspired by those whom media portrays as admirable.
astroturfing: Making a movement or buzz seem like it is grassroots, rising from the bottom up, when it is in fact manufactured by an established group or organization. It is done to give the message more seeming *authenticity*.
authentic, authenticity: The ultimate positive adjective for influencers and other online personalities. It is being genuine and true to one's own nature and not pretending or deceiving others by promoting something that one doesn't genuinely believe in (often for money or fame).
authoritative, authority: When a source, whether a person or organization, can be trusted as being accurate or true on the subject.
avatar: Taken from Hinduism, in the online world it is a character or representation that represents a real-life person. It can be an animated version of the person in a game that looks like the person or it can be customized to reflect the player's preferences, such as their appearance, clothing, accessories, and abilities.
bandwagon effect: The tendency of people to be *swayed* to accept a behavior, custom, or belief because others are doing it. Often the person adapts the crowd's preferences out of *FOMO*.

bias: A prejudice in favor or against a person, thing, or group, usually in a way considered to be unfair.

Boolean operator: A short connecting word used between keywords to help with internet searches, including "and," "or," and "not."

bot: A computer program that can interact with other programs or even humans. Bots do many positive functions, such as repetitive tasks to increase productivity or maintenance, but they also can be used to mislead audiences by disguising as humans, such as liking a post by the thousands to give the false impression that so many humans like it.

brand loyalty: When a consumer stops shopping and comparing brands to automatically stick with purchasing and consuming the same brand over and over again. The consumer may do this because of a belief that a particular brand is superior to others in quality or price, and therefore there is no need to compare, or just out of habit or convenience.

catfish, catfishing: Pretending to be someone you are not or creating a fake *persona* online in order to gain someone's trust, often to then take advantage of the person.

clickbait: Content whose main purpose is to attract attention and entice visitors to click on a link or examine the topic further. It usually appears as headlines or in thumbnails.

confirmation bias: When one collects data or analyzes information subconsciously to conform with one's preexisting opinion or belief. The investigator may only look for examples that support their view or ignore evidence that contradicts their opinion.

content creator: A person who writes or designs the original material that is then available on media platforms such as in a video or on a website.

cookie: A text file or marker placed by a website on computers when you visit them to identify you for when you return and, in some cases, to continuously track what you do online so that your usage data can be collected.

correlation: When two or more things have an association with each other, especially in terms of time. They can happen at the same time or one right after the other. People often draw inferences about how things are related because of correlation, such as that one causes the other, which can be true (people eat more ice cream when it is hot outside) or not (ice cream causes sunburn because both happen more in summer).

credentials: Aspects of a person that give them superior understanding or familiarity with a topic greater than that of the average person. It can be education, experience, achievements, or other aspects of their background that gives them *authority* in the matter.

crowdsourcing: When a large number of people contribute information or opinions from which a general view, opinion, or practice arises.

curate, curation: Editing or choosing select parts of information in order to project a specific image or message. People will curate their life moments for social media to make themselves or their lives appear glamorous and exciting.

cyberbullying: Using technological communication such as text messaging, emails, photos, or any kind of social media post to harass, threaten, humiliate, or intimidate another person. This includes *trolling* and *flaming*, along with threats, malicious pranks or rumors, or getting others to see or act against the person in an unjustified negative way.

disinformation: Incorrect facts intentionally presented or publicized with the intention to mislead or give a false picture of the topic. The intent differs it from *misinformation*.

doom scrolling: The act of continuing to read bad news, usually by continually scrolling down a page. The reader becomes almost transfixed on the barrage of bad news, often becoming depressed or anxious from it all.

Dunning-Kruger effect: A phenomenon identified by psychologists where people with limited knowledge or expertise overestimate their ability and knowledge relative to others. This then tends to make them speak with more assuredness and force despite their lesser *authoritativeness*.

echo chamber: An environment or space, such as an online discussion board, where a person only encounters information or opinions that reflect and reinforce their own views, seeming to verify the person's opinion by an outside source. This can amplify the apparent strength of the single point of view and its hold on the person.

eye candy: Visual images that are superficially attractive and entertaining to grab your immediate attention, but often lack intellectual depth. A form of *clickbait*.

fake intimacy: When a celebrity enhances their appeal by appearing to establish a more personal and intimate connection with their fans and audience.

filter bubble: A situation where online algorithms personalize their results based on your past behavior and preferences to give you information and opinions like your own. This is often done by eliminating or deprioritizing information and opinions the algorithm determines are contrary or different from yours. The effect is to put a person in an *echo chamber*, overly reinforcing their perspective by making it seem more universal and reducing exposure to other perspectives.

finsta: A portmanteau deriving from "fake Insta(gram)." It is a private social media account, often of a minor, that is only shared with friends so that the owner can be more forthcoming or engage in conversation and activity that would be disapproved of by parents and others. To hide the finsta, the person creates a **rinsta** (real Insta[gram]) that is their *persona* for the public or their parents.

flaming: More of a dated term nowadays, it is when a person responds to a post, such as a comment, email, or text, with an excessive attack of insults and personal comments against the original poster. It is a form of *cyberbullying*.

FOMO: An acronym for "fear of missing out," it's a bad or uneasy feeling that one is not being included in a popular trend, which makes the person want to know about and participate in that trend whether they are actually interested in it or not.

formal relationship: When one interacts with someone as part of someone's societal role or profession, such as a doctor or teacher.

Googleganger: Someone who has the same name as you, so that the two of you might be confused online, such as in searches.

grab and go (GAG): A technique whereby someone seeking information online or using a search engine takes the first result that pops up and automatically accepts it as the best answer without verifying or even considering its validity or other search results.

hedge, hedging: Adding qualifying or limiting words so there is wiggle room to claim that the statement was not made as an absolute promise.

heuristic: A mental shortcut or rule of thumb used to make decisions more quickly or to easily understand, categorize, and respond to a situation, especially choices.

humblebrag: A post or statement that seems to invoke modesty or self-deprecation, but the real purpose is to brag about an achievement.

impromptu: When something is done without being planned, spontaneously.

incidental relationship: When one interacts with another person one time or briefly, such as with a sales clerk or someone you bump into. There is no lasting social bond.

influencer: Someone who uses their popularity to affect large-scale decisions in society. The decisions can be personal choices, such as fashion, or be things on a broader scale, such as politics. Most influencers today have social media platforms from which they *sway* large numbers of people by commenting on, using, or displaying an issue, item, or logo.

innuendo: The use of indirect or vague statements to suggest or imply something, usually negative, but without saying it directly.

IRL: Short for "in real life." This is a common shorthand used to distinguish what happens in the physical world versus online, such as "IRL you don't get unlimited do-overs."

juxtaposition: Putting things side by side so that the observer will compare or contrast the things. One could put up a picture of two hated people and then a third person to imply the viewer should see the third person in the same way, using *innuendo*.

KGOY: An acronym for "kids getting older, younger," it describes how issues and choices, some serious, are coming into kids' lives at a younger age than they did for previous generations.

malware: Software or program designed to damage, disrupt, or steal data from someone else. Often used in *phishing* or *smishing*.

meme: A short text, picture, graphic, or other message designed to be shared online and, if possible, go *viral*.

misinformation: "Facts" asserted that are not actually true or are incomplete or presented out of context. They can *sway* a person to draw an incorrect conclusion. Misinformation may be presented unintentionally, as opposed to *disinformation*.

nudge: In behavioral economics, a suggestion or emphasis that encourages people to choose option B over option A. It is not a command to choose one in particular, but it can be the situation is set up to increase the likelihood of choosing B or to decrease the likelihood of choosing A. As we use them, nudges are supplied at the moment of choice, as opposed to *sways*.

opportunity cost: When one chooses, such as option A over option B, the opportunity cost is the good or benefit one would have received had one chosen option B. Its sacrifice becomes a cost of choosing option A.

othering: Also called **theming,** it is when we mentally put people who are different from us, or who have different tastes, into one group. We then think of them as one mass, no longer as individuals. They then seem more threatening and less human, which can lead to negative perception and mistreatment of them. Othering is often a precursor to prejudice, verbal abuse, and physical violence toward people because we no longer see their humanity.

oversharing: Revealing too much of one's personal life to the point of making one's audience feel uncomfortable.

parasocial relationship: A one-sided social connection, where one person feels an *affinity* for the other, while the other party is mostly unaware of the other's existence.

peer-reviewed: When an article or other publication has been assessed and critiqued by others in the same field for accuracy before it is published, adding to its *authoritativeness*.

persona: An image or personality a person presents publicly. It may be the same as their true, authentic self or it may be very different, but it is the personality that people associate with the person.

personal celebrity: When a person, such as an *influencer*, has a significant following among a specific niche audience rather than the general public.

It can cultivate a bonding within that group, as the in-crowd feels special for following that influencer.

phishing: An email scam in which a scammer send an email that looks like it is from a reputable company and then tries to get the receiver to give out personal data or click on a link that can extract the data or put *malware* on the receiver's device.

poisoning the well: A fallacy in arguing in which a person seeks to discredit people with a particular view, such as claiming anyone who believes that must be "an idiot," "blind to reality," or "corrupt." It is often done before the other side is heard so that people will already be against the other person's point of view.

pop: A description used in entertainment, it is when something makes people stop and react with a wondrous "Whoa!" fascination that keeps them interested. It's often a surprise or a "I can't believe they did that!" moment in the entertainment, even if it is commonly preplanned by the presenters.

posing: Dressing or acting in an artificial way to try to give a false impression of who you are. Unsuccessfully trying to pass oneself off in a way that is not *authentic* or who you truly are.

privacy settings: The options that allow an account owner to control who can access and view their personal information, activities, and posts on their devices and online.

re-bias: A technique to gather a balanced perspective on a topic by gathering many opinions, even if many are biased. In theory, the sum total of *biased* opinions from multiple sources can provide a more centered, objective, and comprehensive understanding.

rhetorical question: Asking a question where the answer is implied. The question is not asked to get an answer so much as to make a statement, such as "Aren't I honest?"

sample size: A part of a whole used to assess the greater whole. It can be an object, such as one apple to judge the bushel; a group of people to make judgments about the group they represent; or a time period to make an estimate how the rest of the time is used.

sampling error: Occurs when one makes false judgments or conclusions based on a sample that does not accurately represent the greater whole. (3)

smishing: *Phishing*, but through text messaging rather than email.

social calculus: The act of simultaneously having to mentally be directly engaged and observingly distanced from a social interaction in order to evaluate the situation and decide how to act. It might be deciding in the moment whether a comment was meant honestly or sarcastically, and how you should respond to it. The process can be tiring because one has to both participate in and assess what is going on at the same time, causing tension and discomfort.

social relationship: The connections that exist between people who have recurring interactions that are perceived by the participants to have personal meaning. Whether or not that includes a one-way relationship, such as a *parasocial relationship*, is subject to debate. Social relationships also stand apart from *incidental relationships* and *formal relationships*.

sock puppet: As opposed to a *bot*, this is an account, such as on social media, run by a real person but in a disguised manner, usually as part of multiple accounts, to magnify the person's opinion to make it seem like many share it. A seller might create sock puppets to give multiple praising reviews of their own product.

stakeholder: Someone who has something to gain or lose in a decision made by someone. They often are not the one making the actual decision, but they are affected by the choice.

stan: An obsessively devoted fan of a celebrity, group, or show, often leading to overzealous behavior in support of the celebrity, group, or show.

straw man fallacy: When a person making a counterargument reduces the other side to an overly simplified or distorted form to make it easy to refute or put down, then claims they defeated the original counterargument.

sway: An internal or external influence such as past experiences, cultural background, advertising, and personal beliefs that over time shapes a person's overall preferences and biases, leading them toward certain choices over others. Choosers thus arrive at a decision moment already preferring one choice over another, even before the effect of *nudges*.

trending: Currently popular or widely discussed, often online and especially on social media.

trolling: Deliberately seeking to upset or antagonize a person on the internet by posting inflammatory, nonsensical, outrageous, or otherwise offensive comments. Trolling is one form of *cyberbullying*.

videogenic: Having an appearance or manner that is appealing in videos, as telegenic was for television and photogenic for photographs.

viral: Online, when something becomes quickly popular, is *trending*, and is shared from person to person.

Bibliography

Armstrong, Martin. "Kids on Social Media." Statista, April 6, 2022. https://www.statista.com/chart/27200/kids-on-social-media-uk-survey.

August, Kristin J., and Karen S. Rook. "Social Relationships." In *Encyclopedia of Behavioral Medicine*, 1838–42. New York: Springer, 2013. https://doi.org/10.1007/978-1-4419-1005-9_59.

Burch, Kelly. "How Does Social Media Affect Teenagers? Understanding the Mental Health Impact—and Why It's Not All Bad." Insider, May 16, 2022. https://www.insider.com/guides/health/mental-health/how-does-social-media-affect-teenagers.

Common Sense. "The Common Sense Census: Media Use by Tweens and Teens, 2021." https://www.commonsensemedia.org/sites/default/files/research/report/2022-infographic-8-18-census-web-final-release_0.pdf.

Danckert, James, and John D. Eastwood. "Boredom across the Lifespan." British Psychological Society, June 8, 2020. https://www.bps.org.uk/psychologist/boredom-across-lifespan.

Dixon, S. "Age U.S. Parents Believe Is Appropriate for Kids Social Media Use 2022." Statista, August 15, 2022. https://www.statista.com/statistics/1326635/appropriate-age-for-kids-own-social-media-account-us.

———. "U.S. Facebook Users by Age and Gender 2022." Statista, January 9, 2023. https://www.statista.com/statistics/187041/us-user-age-distribution-on-facebook.

———. "U.S. Young Users Daily Media Activities during the COVID-19 Pandemic 2021, by Age." Statista, January 10, 2022. https://www.statista.com/statistics/1281555/us-kids-teens-daily-activities-coronavirus-by-age.

Forster, Madison. "How Many Kids Give Away Information to Strangers?" Savvy Cyber Kids, July 21, 2022. https://savvycyberkids.org/2022/07/21/how-many-kids-give-away-information-to-strangers.

Founders Online. "Adams' Argument for the Defense: 3–4 December 1770." National Archives, n.d. https://founders.archives.gov/documents/Adams/05-03-02-0001-0004-0016.

Global Witness. "TikTok and Facebook Fail to Detect Election Disinformation in the US, While YouTube Succeeds." October 21, 2022. https://www.globalwitness.org/en/campaigns/digital-threats/tiktok-and-facebook-fail-detect-election-disinformation-us-while-youtube-succeeds.

Google Trends. "Influencer." n.d. https://trends.google.com/trends/explore?date=all&geo=US&q=influencer.

Grossman, David. "On This Day 25 Years Ago, the Web Became Public Domain." *Popular Mechanics*, April 30, 2018. https://www.popularmechanics.com/culture/web/a20104417/www-public-domain.

Hill, Jay. "How Social Media Is Making You Feel Bad about Yourself Every Day." LifeHack, June 12, 2017. https://www.lifehack.org/600150/how-social-media-fuels-jealousy.

Horton, Donald, and Richard Wohl. "Mass Communication and Para-Social Interaction." *Psychiatry* 19, no. 3 (August 1956): 215–29. https://doi.org/10.1080/00332747.1956.11023049.

Instagram. "Continuing to Make Instagram Safer for the Youngest Members of Our Community," March 17, 2021. https://about.instagram.com/blog/announcements/continuing-to-make-instagram-safer-for-the-youngest-members-of-our-community.

Iqbal, Mansoor. "Instagram Revenue and Usage Statistics (2018)." Business of Apps, March 8, 2021. https://www.businessofapps.com/data/instagram-statistics.

———. "Snapchat Revenue and Usage Statistics (2019)." Business of Apps, August 8, 2017. https://www.businessofapps.com/data/snapchat-statistics.

———. "TikTok Revenue and Usage Statistics (2021)." Business of Apps. Business of Apps, November 11, 2022. https://www.businessofapps.com/data/tik-tok-statistics.

Johnson, Benjamin. "Look Up, Look Down: Articulating Inputs and Outputs of Social Media Social Comparison." *Journal of Communication Technology* 4, no. 1 (2021). https://doi.org/10.51548/joctec-2021-003.

Kamenetz, Anya. "Right Wing Hate Groups Are Recruiting Video Gamers." NPR, November 5, 2018. https://www.npr.org/2018/11/05/660642531/right-wing-hate-groups-are-recruiting-video-gamers.

Loveland, Mariel. "Teens Would Rather Text and Chat Online with Their Friends Than Hang Out in Real Life, Study Says." Insider, September 12, 2018. https://www.insider.com/study-teens-would-rather-text-with-friends-than-hang-out-in-real-life-2018-9.

Maravilla, Rafael. "Kids as Young as 8 Are Using Social Media More Than Ever, Study Finds." PACEsConnection, March 25, 2022 (originally published in the *New York Times*, March 24, 2022). https://www.pacesconnection.com/blog/kids-as-young-as-8-are-using-social-media-more-than-ever-study-finds-nytimes-com.

Matsa, Katerina Eva. "More Americans Are Getting News on TikTok, Bucking the Trend on Other Social Media Sites." Pew Research Center, October 21, 2022. https://www.pewresearch.org/fact-tank/2022/10/21/more-americans-are-getting-news-on-tiktok-bucking-the-trend-on-other-social-media-sites.

McEvoy, Jemima. "Facebook Internal Research Found Instagram Can Be Very Harmful to Young Girls, Report Says." *Forbes*, September 14, 2021. https://www.forbes.com/sites/jemimamcevoy/2021/09/14/facebook-internal-research-found-instagram-can-be-very-harmful-to-young-girls-report-says.

Microsoft on the Issues. "How Old Is Too Young to Go Online?" October 14, 2013. https://blogs.microsoft.com/on-the-issues/2013/10/14/how-old-is-too-young-to-go-online.

Morganelli, Marie. "When People Compare Themselves to Their Social Media Friends, It Can Help or Hurt Their Feelings." UF College of Journalism and Communications, May 13, 2021. https://www.jou.ufl.edu/insights/when-people-compare-themselves-to-their-social-media-friends-it-can-help-or-hurt-their-feelings.

National Center for Education Statistics. "Children's Internet Access at Home." May 2021. https://nces.ed.gov/programs/coe/indicator/cch/home-internet-access.

National Poll on Children's Health. "Sharing Too Soon? Children and Social Media Apps." C. H. Mott Children's Hospital, October 18, 2021. https://mottpoll.org/reports/sharing-too-soon-children-and-social-media-apps.

Nelson, Maya. "The Dark Side of Stan Culture." *Stanford Daily*, August 24, 2021. https://stanforddaily.com/2021/08/23/the-dark-side-of-stan-culture.

Newton, Tony. "Confusing COPPA Terms on YouTube Lead to More Questions for the FTC." Scalefluence.com, February 6, 2020. https://www.scalefluence.com/confusing-coppa-terms-on-youtube.

Ofcom. Home page. Accessed December 14, 2018. https://www.ofcom.org.uk.

———. "A Third of Children Have False Social Media Age of 18+." October 11, 2022. https://www.ofcom.org.uk/news-centre/2022/a-third-of-children-have-false-social-media-age-of-18.

ParentsTogether Action. "Parent Advisory: 2021 Sets Records for Child Sexual Abuse Online; 3x Increase in Sexual Images of 7-10 Year Olds." January 18, 2022. https://parentstogetheraction.org/2022/01/18/parent-advisory-2021-sets-records-for-child-sexual-abuse-online.

Pariser, Eli. "Beware Online 'Filter Bubbles.'" TED, March 2011. https://www.ted.com/talks/eli_pariser_beware_online_filter_bubbles?language=en.

Petrosyan, Ani. "Age Distribution of Internet Users Worldwide 20211." Statista, February 23, 2023. https://www.statista.com/statistics/272365/age-distribution-of-internet-users-worldwide.

Quaker Oats. "Helper of Hearts." 2023. https://www.quakeroats.com/extraordinary-oats/keep-your-heart-healthy.

Rideout, Victoria, and Susannah Fox. *Digital Health Practices, Social Media Use, and Mental Well-Being among Teens and Young Adults in the U.S.* Hopelab and Well Being Trust, 2018. https://assets.hopelab.org/wp-content/uploads/2020/08/a-national-survey-by-hopelab-and-well-being-trust-2018.pdf.

Rideout, V., A. Peebles, S. Mann, and M. B. Robb. *The Common Sense Census: Media Use by Tweens and Teens, 2021*. San Francisco: Common Sense, 2022. https://www.commonsensemedia.org/sites/default/files/research/report/8-18-census-integrated-report-final-web_0.pdf.

Rogers, Kristen. "Children under 10 Are Using Social Media. Parents Can Help Them Stay Safe Online." CNN, October 18, 2021. https://www.cnn.com/2021/10/18/health/children-social-media-apps-use-poll-wellness/index.html.

Roos, Dave. "How Paul Revere's Engraving of the Boston Massacre Rallied the Patriot Cause." History Channel, August 16, 2021. https://www.history.com/news/paul-revere-engraving-boston-massacre.

Sha, Peng, and Xiaoyu Dong. "Research on Adolescents Regarding the Indirect Effect of Depression, Anxiety, and Stress between TikTok Use Disorder and Memory Loss." *International Journal of Environmental Research and Public Health* 18, no. 16 (August 21, 2021): 8820. https://doi.org/10.3390/ijerph18168820.

Shepherd, Jack. "21 Essential Snapchat Statistics You Need to Know in 2022." *The Social Shepherd*, January 3, 2023. https://thesocialshepherd.com/blog/snapchat-statistics.

Tiggemann, Marika, and Amy Slater. "NetTweens: The Internet and Body Image Concerns in Preteenage Girls." *The Journal of Early Adolescence* 34, no. 5 (September 5, 2013): 606–20. https://doi.org/10.1177/0272431613501083.

Villano, Matt. "Why Hanging Out Face-to-Face Still Matters." CNN, June 8, 2021. https://www.cnn.com/2021/06/07/health/face-to-face-brain-wellness-scn/index.html.

Wikipedia. "On the Internet, Nobody Knows You're a Dog." Last modified January 10, 2020. https://en.wikipedia.org/wiki/On_the_Internet,_nobody_knows_you%27re_a_dog.

About the Authors

Jim Wasserman is a former business litigation attorney and, for over twenty years, media literacy, economics, and humanities teacher. He has written extensively on education generally and media literacy specifically, including a three-book series on how to introduce media literacy to elementary, middle, and high school students.

Jiab Wasserman is a former industrial engineer and bank executive, becoming a vice president at Bank of America. Since retiring, she has become a trailblazer in advocating for gender, ethnic, and immigrant equity in the workplace and in education. She has written about the financial world and financial practices for several years and continues to be a regular contributor on the subject.

Milton Keynes UK
Ingram Content Group UK Ltd.
UKHW011442141223
434363UK00012B/111